Collins

AF662443

# English Expert

## COURSEBOOK 4

Name:..................................................................................

Grade:......................    Section:...................................

I am an Indian author of British origin. I wrote my first novel at the age of 17. I went on to write more than 500 short stories, including nearly 70 children's books over a period of seven decades. Who am I?......................

Safa Abdul Razak | Sonia Duggal

HarperCollins*Publishers*

*Publishing operations in 17 countries and 120+ imprints globally*

William Collins' dream of knowledge for all began with the publication of his first book in 1819. A self-educated mill worker, he not only enriched millions of lives, but also founded a flourishing publishing house. Today, staying true to this spirit, Collins books are packed with inspiration, innovation and practical expertise. They place you at the centre of a world of possibility and give you exactly what you need to explore it.

Published by Collins Learning
An imprint of HarperCollins*Publishers* India
Building No. 10, Tower A, 4th Floor, DLF Cyber City, Gurugram, Haryana 122002, India

First edition: 2024
Reprint edition: 2025
ISBN: 978-93-6213-925-2

The publishers would like to thank the following reviewers for their suggestions and inputs:

**Renu Arora**
Saint Margaret Senior Secondary School, New Delhi

**Shalini Sharma**
Mother's International School

**Radhika Tadepalli**
Principal,
Modern Academy Senior Secondary School, Ghaziabad

Printed and bound by Thomson Press India Ltd

Browse the complete Collins catalogue at www.collins.in.
For any queries/feedback, please write to us at SCHOOLSUPPORT@harpercollins.co.in.

# Preface

*English Expert* is a new multi-skill course in English that aims to address the needs of the learners, as underlined in the National Curriculum Framework (NCF) 2023, one of whose underlying principles is a concerted shift towards competency-based learning. This series is distinct in its inclusion of curricular goals, mapped to the respective competencies outlined by the new NCF. It focuses on literacy through thoughtfully curated content, exercises, and activities that will help to develop the 3Hs – Curious Heads, Skilled Hands, and Compassionate Hearts.

Grades 1, 3, and 6 include bridge chapters that act as a pedagogical link between the Foundational, Middle, and the Preparatory Stages. The formal requirements of language are integrated with the appreciation of literature-rich content. This is done through a combination of the communicative and the language-through-literature approaches towards language acquisition.

Care has been taken to include India-focused content and activities adhering to the principles of experiential learning and mindfulness. Additionally, the series aims to develop 21st century skills and awareness about the United Nations' Sustainable Development Goals in learners. It also fosters art integration through activities.

**Coursebooks 1–8** comprise a mix of prose, poetry, and drama authored by Indian and global writers, based on themes like self and family, climate change, gender, and inclusivity. The exercises include factual, analytical, life skills, and value-based questions. Grades 6–8 include a HOTS-based comprehension section, in keeping with the latest assessment pattern. A self-assessment at the beginning of Coursebooks 2–8 acts as a useful diagnostic tool.

**Language Companions 1–8** comprise extensive reading comprehension, composition, and integrated grammar and vocabulary tasks. It is designed for practice and reinforcement of the concepts taught in the Coursebooks. All topics are mapped to the respective Coursebooks and can be used for independent practice. The Language Companions for classes 3 to 8 also include SAFAL (Structured Assessments for Analyzing Learning) assessments.

**Supplementary Readers 1–8** have been designed in keeping with the NCF's focus on 'drop everything and read'. The simple yet high-quality reading material has been curated to inculcate the habit of reading in learners. These books will introduce them to a wide variety of literary genres by both Indian and global authors.

**Teacher's Resource Books 1–8** contain lesson plans, additional worksheets, listening transcripts for listening exercises, and answer keys for the Coursebooks, Language Companions, and additional worksheets.

**Collins DigiSuite 1–8** comprises multimedia e-books, animations of the reading passages in the Coursebooks, interactivities based on the vocabulary and grammar sections, and a Test Generator for the creation of customized assignments and question papers.

**Icons** The series prepares learners with the various skills outlined in the NCF 2023. These are tagged with easily recognizable icons.

**Twenty-first Century Skills** ensure that today's students can thrive in an ever-changing world.

Collaboration · Communication · Creativity · Critical Thinking · Initiative · Leadership · Media Literacy · Productivity · Flexibility · Information Literacy · Social Skills · Technology Literacy · Innovation

**India-Focused** content puts the spotlight on the heritage, culture, customs, history and geography of the Indian subcontinent.

**Art Integrated Learning** is a pedagogic model that integrates the fine arts, performing arts, and photography into teaching.

The **Sustainable Development Goals**, adopted by the United Nations in 2015, are a collection of 17 inter-linked goals designed to achieve a sustainable future for all by 2030.

SUSTAINABLE DEVELOPMENT GOALS

# Key Features

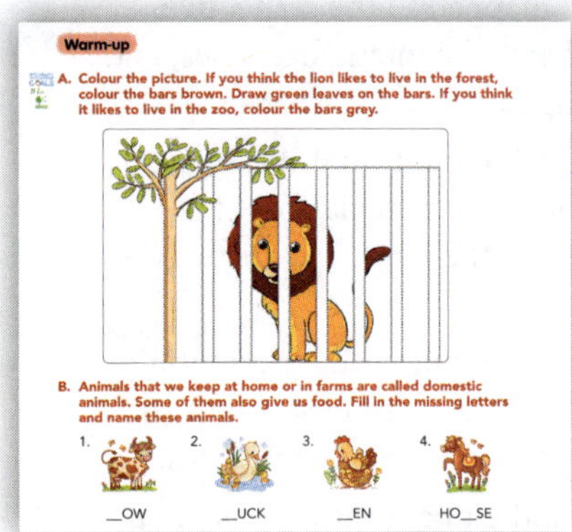
Warm-up
A. Colour the picture. If you think the lion likes to live in the forest, colour the bars brown. Draw green leaves on the bars. If you think it likes to live in the zoo, colour the bars grey.
B. Animals that we keep at home or in farms are called domestic animals. Some of them also give us food. Fill in the missing letters and name these animals.
1. __OW 2. __UCK 3. __EN 4. HO__SE

**Warm-up** has theme-based activities.

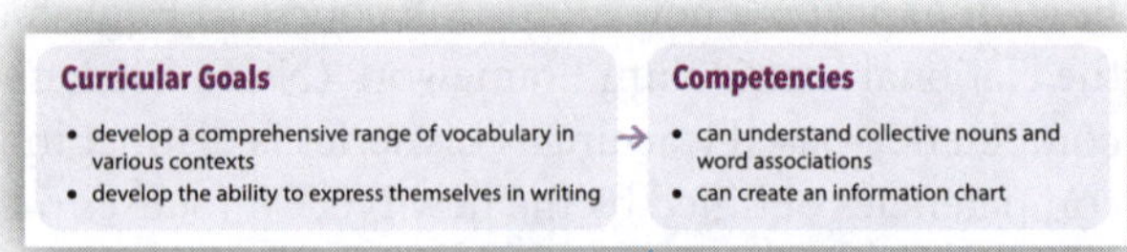

| Curricular Goals | Competencies |
|---|---|
| • develop a comprehensive range of vocabulary in various contexts<br>• develop the ability to express themselves in writing | • can understand collective nouns and word associations<br>• can create an information chart |

**Curricular Goals** are mapped to the respective **Competencies** outlined in the NCF 2023.

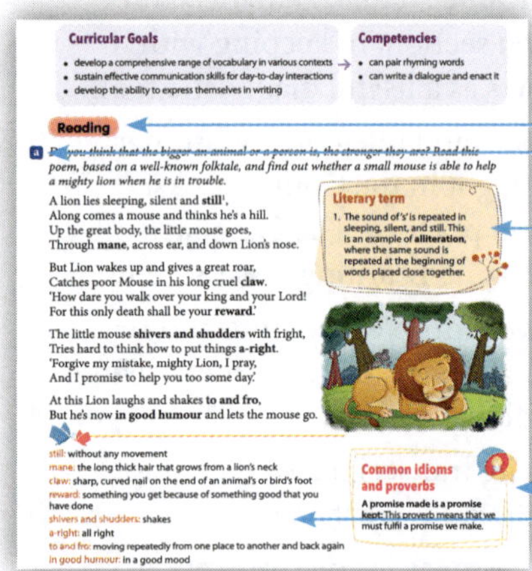
Curricular Goals: • develop a comprehensive range of vocabulary in various contexts • sustain effective communication skills for day-to-day interactions • develop the ability to express themselves in writing
Competencies: • can pair rhyming words • can write a dialogue and enact it
Reading
Do you think that the bigger an animal or a person is, the stronger they are? Read this poem, based on a well-known folktale, and find out whether a small mouse is able to help a mighty lion when he is in trouble.
A lion lies sleeping, silent and still[1],
Along comes a mouse and thinks he's a hill.
Up the great body, the little mouse goes,
Through mane, across ear, and down Lion's nose.
But Lion wakes up and gives a great roar,
Catches poor Mouse in his long cruel claw.
'How dare you walk over your king and your Lord!
For this only death shall be your reward.'
The little mouse shivers and shudders with fright,
Tries hard to think how to put things a-right.
'Forgive my mistake, mighty Lion, I pray,
And I promise to help you too some day.'
At this Lion laughs and shakes to and fro,
But he's now in good humour and lets the mouse go.
Literary term: 1. The sound of 's' is repeated in sleeping, silent, and still. This is an example of alliteration, where the same sound is repeated at the beginning of words placed close together.
still: without any movement
mane: the long thick hair that grows from a lion's neck
claw: sharp, curved nail on the end of an animal's or bird's foot
reward: something you get because of something good that you have done
shivers and shudders: shakes
a-right: all right
to and fro: moving repeatedly from one place to another and back again
in good humour: in a good mood
Common idioms and proverbs: A promise made is a promise kept: This proverb means that we must fulfil a promise we make.

**Reading** comprises a rich variety of texts by global and Indian writers.

All reading passages are accompanied by an animation in **DigiSuite** and tagged by an icon. a

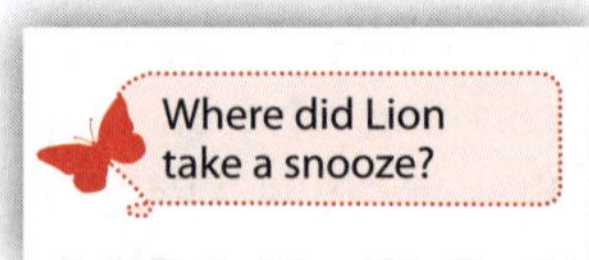
Where did Lion take a snooze?

While-reading **in-text questions** check factual understanding.

**Cross-curricular corner, Literary terms, Common idioms and proverbs** have additional trivia, explanations of figures of speech, and idiomatic structures.

**Glossary** includes contextual meanings of difficult words.

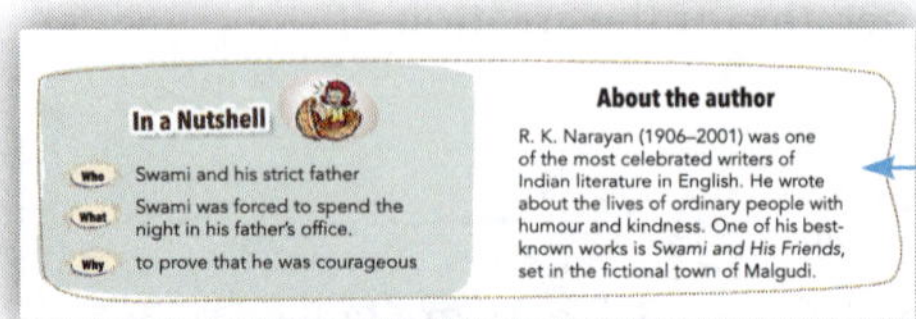
In a Nutshell
Who: Swami and his strict father
What: Swami was forced to spend the night in his father's office.
Why: to prove that he was courageous
About the author
R. K. Narayan (1906–2001) was one of the most celebrated writers of Indian literature in English. He wrote about the lives of ordinary people with humour and kindness. One of his best-known works is *Swami and His Friends*, set in the fictional town of Malgudi.

**In a Nutshell** is a useful revision tool which recapitulates the key aspects of the text.

**About the author/poet/playwright** includes a brief biography of the author/poet.

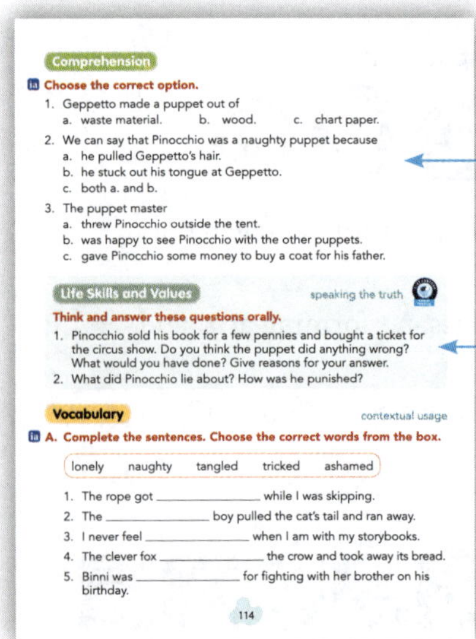
Comprehension
Choose the correct option.
1. Geppetto made a puppet out of
a. waste material. b. wood. c. chart paper.
2. We can say that Pinocchio was a naughty puppet because
a. he pulled Geppetto's hair.
b. he stuck out his tongue at Geppetto.
c. both a. and b.
3. The puppet master
a. threw Pinocchio outside the tent.
b. was happy to see Pinocchio with the other puppets.
c. gave Pinocchio some money to buy a coat for his father.
Life Skills and Values — speaking the truth
Think and answer these questions orally.
1. Pinocchio sold his book for a few pennies and bought a ticket for the circus show. Do you think the puppet did anything wrong? What would you have done? Give reasons for your answer.
2. What did Pinocchio lie about? How was he punished?
Vocabulary — contextual usage
A. Complete the sentences. Choose the correct words from the box.
lonely naughty tangled tricked ashamed
1. The rope got ________ while I was skipping.
2. The ________ boy pulled the cat's tail and ran away.
3. I never feel ________ when I am with my storybooks.
4. The clever fox ________ the crow and took away its bread.
5. Binni was ________ for fighting with her brother on his birthday.
114

**Comprehension** checks factual understanding through 'wh-' and objective questions of various types.

**Life Skills and Values** has inferential questions on values and interpersonal skills.

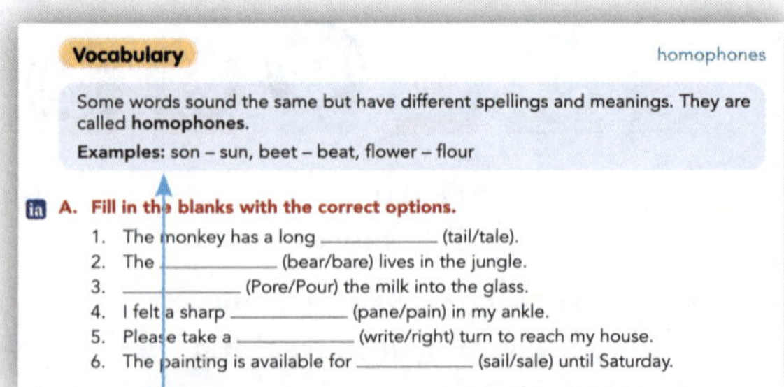
Vocabulary — homophones
Some words sound the same but have different spellings and meanings. They are called **homophones**.
**Examples:** son – sun, beet – beat, flower – flour
A. Fill in the blanks with the correct options.
1. The monkey has a long ________ (tail/tale).
2. The ________ (bear/bare) lives in the jungle.
3. ________ (Pore/Pour) the milk into the glass.
4. I felt a sharp ________ (pane/pain) in my ankle.
5. Please take a ________ (write/right) turn to reach my house.
6. The painting is available for ________ (sail/sale) until Saturday.

**Vocabulary** includes exercises on contextual usage, modes of language acquisition and figures of speech.

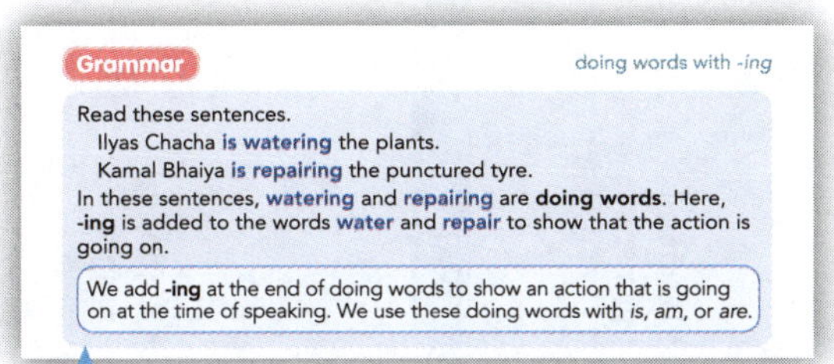

Grammar — doing words with *-ing*

Read these sentences.

Ilyas Chacha **is watering** the plants.

Kamal Bhaiya **is repairing** the punctured tyre.

In these sentences, **watering** and **repairing** are **doing words**. Here, **-ing** is added to the words **water** and **repair** to show that the action is going on.

We add **-ing** at the end of doing words to show an action that is going on at the time of speaking. We use these doing words with *is*, *am*, or *are*.

**Grammar** includes graded practice tasks accompanied by simple explanations.

**Study Skills** includes graded phonics, spelling, and dictionary activities.

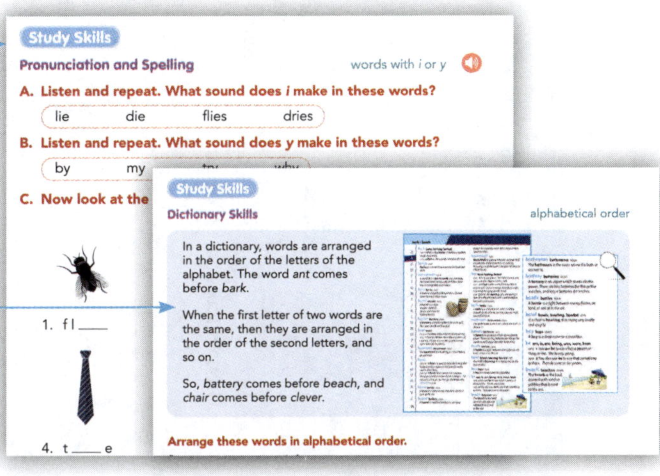

Study Skills

Pronunciation and Spelling — words with *i* or *y*

A. Listen and repeat. What sound does *i* make in these words?

lie die flies dries

B. Listen and repeat. What sound does *y* make in these words?

by my

C. Now look at the

1. f l ____

4. t ____ e

Study Skills

Dictionary Skills — alphabetical order

In a dictionary, words are arranged in the order of the letters of the alphabet. The word *ant* comes before *bark*.

When the first letter of two words are the same, then they are arranged in the order of the second letters, and so on.

So, *battery* comes before *beach*, and *chair* comes before *clever*.

Arrange these words in alphabetical order.

B. How does each member of the family help Bala's mother? Look at the pictures. Match each picture with the person.

Grandpa Father Grandma Bala

Exercises available as interactivities on **DigiSuite** are tagged with an icon.

**Listening** covers aural comprehension activities, as well as word and sentence-based **Dictation** tasks.

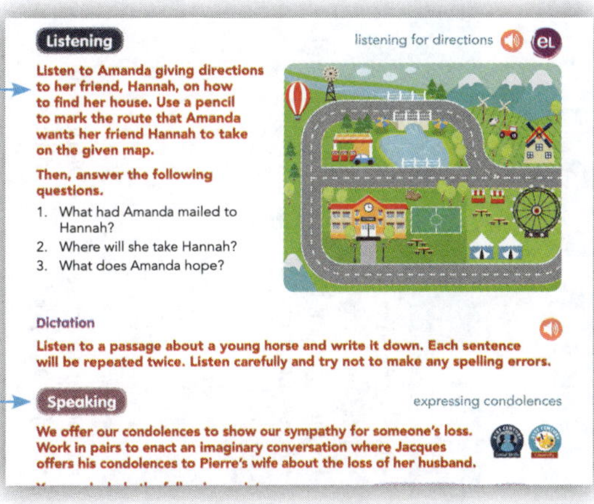

Listening — listening for directions

Listen to Amanda giving directions to her friend, Hannah, on how to find her house. Use a pencil to mark the route that Amanda wants her friend Hannah to take on the given map.

Then, answer the following questions.

1. What had Amanda mailed to Hannah?
2. Where will she take Hannah?
3. What does Amanda hope?

Dictation

Listen to a passage about a young horse and write it down. Each sentence will be repeated twice. Listen carefully and try not to make any spelling errors.

Speaking — expressing condolences

We offer our condolences to show our sympathy for someone's loss. Work in pairs to enact an imaginary conversation where Jacques offers his condolences to Pierre's wife about the loss of her husband.

**Speaking** includes role plays, conversation practice and public speaking tasks through solo, pair and group work. It also covers financial literacy tasks.

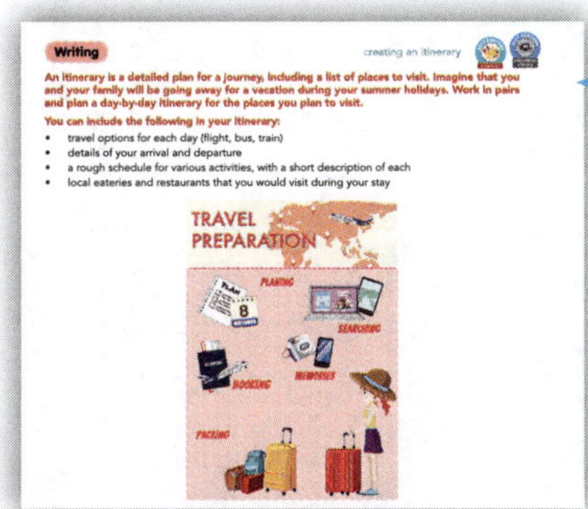

Writing — creating an itinerary

An itinerary is a detailed plan for a journey, including a list of places to visit. Imagine that you and your family will be going away for a vacation during your summer holidays. Work in pairs and plan a day-by-day itinerary for the places you plan to visit.

You can include the following in your itinerary:

- travel options for each day (flight, bus, train)
- details of your arrival and departure
- a rough schedule for various activities, with a short description of each
- local eateries and restaurants that you would visit during your stay



**Writing** includes graded and free composition. Poetry chapters include **Activity**, a hands-on creative task.

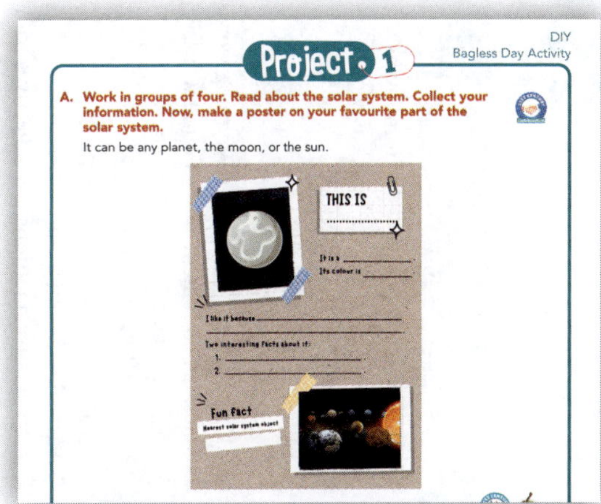

Project 1 — DIY Bagless Day Activity

A. Work in groups of four. Read about the solar system. Collect your information. Now, make a poster on your favourite part of the solar system.

It can be any planet, the moon, or the sun.



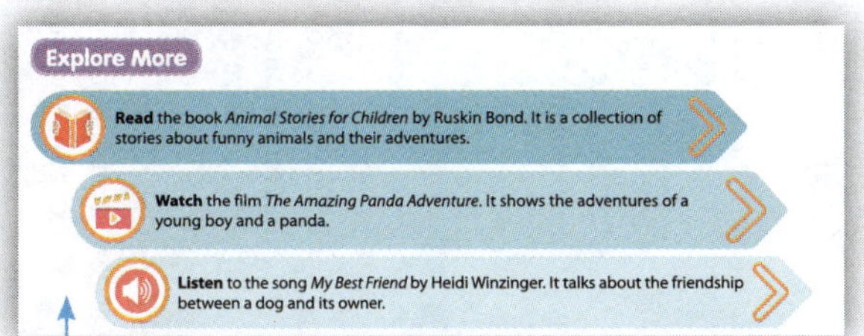

Explore More

**Read** the book *Animal Stories for Children* by Ruskin Bond. It is a collection of stories about funny animals and their adventures.

**Watch** the film *The Amazing Panda Adventure*. It shows the adventures of a young boy and a panda.

**Listen** to the song *My Best Friend* by Heidi Winzinger. It talks about the friendship between a dog and its owner.

**Explore More** has suggestions for further reading, watching and listening to encourage learners to delve further into the theme of the reading text.

**Projects** cover cross-curricular activities aligned to the unit themes. They also include 'bagless day' activities.

# Detailed Contents

| Unit | Chapter Name | Reading Comprehension | Vocabulary | Grammar | Study Skills | Listening | Speaking | Writing | Activity |
|---|---|---|---|---|---|---|---|---|---|
| **I. Imagination** | 1. A Different Kind of Dragon | • Factual questions<br>• Flowchart<br>• Inferential and extrapolative questions | • Homonyms<br>• Crossword | • Types of nouns<br>• Material nouns<br>• Simple present tense<br>• Present continuous tense | • Spelling: commonly misspelt words | • Listening to a passage and sequencing | • Giving, accepting, and refusing an invitation | • Writing a thank-you note | |
| | 2. *Oliphaunt* | • MCQ<br>• Reference to context<br>• Inferential and extrapolative questions | • Rhyming words<br>• Sound words | | | | | | • Dumb charades<br>• Writing a notice |
| **II. Our Country** | 3. North, South, East, West | • MCQ<br>• Factual, inferential, and extrapolative questions | • Prefixes: *un-*, *dis-*, *re-*<br>• Adjectives with sufffixes *-ing* and *-less* | • Types of adjectives<br>• Subject and predicate | • Dictionary skills: words of Indian origin | • Listening to a telephone conversation and gap filling | • Group discussion | • Writing an informal letter | |
| | 4. *Land of Glories* | • Reference to context<br>• Factual, inferential, and extrapolative questions | • Word pairs<br>• Alliteration | | | | | | • Reciting a poem with correct stress |
| **III. Adventure** | 5. The Hound in the Red Jersey | • True and false<br>• Factual, inferential, and extrapolative questions | • Similes<br>• Regular and irregular verbs | • Transitive and intransitive verbs<br>• Punctuation: comma, full stop, capital letters, exclamation mark | • Pronunciation: Words with *al* sound | • Listening to a passage followed by MCQ | • Giving a speech | • Making a diary entry | |
| | 6. Robin Hood Tricks the Sheriff | • True and false<br>• Factual, inferential, and extrapolative questions | • Synonyms<br>• Compound words | • Using *who* or *which*<br>• Articles: *a*, *an*, *the* | • Spelling: double-letter words | • Listening to a poem and gap filling<br>• Dictation of a short passage | • Making guesses | • Writing a paragraph | |
| Project 1 (DIY and bagless day activity) • Making a collage • Designing a treasure map for a treasure hunt game | | | | | | | | | |
| **IV. Food and History** | 7. *Eating Words* | • MCQ<br>• Reference to context<br>• Inferential and extrapolative questions | • Antonyms<br>• Analogies | | | | | | • Limericks |
| | 8. Around the World with a Chilli | • Gap filling<br>• Factual, inferential, and extrapolative questions | • Homophones<br>• Words related to food | • Prepositions<br>• Subject–verb agreement | • Dictionary skills: headwords | • Listening to a passage and matching facts | • Asking and answering questions with the correct intonation | • Writing a recipe | |

| | | | | | | | | | |
|---|---|---|---|---|---|---|---|---|---|
| **V. In the Forest** | 9. Trapped by a Tiger | • True and False<br>• Factual, inferential, and extrapolative questions | • Contextual usage<br>• Animal idioms | • Simple past tense<br>• Past continuous tense | • Pronunciation: long and short *o* sounds; *oa* and *ow* sounds | • Listening and marking directions on a map | • Narrating a short story based on a proverb | • Writing a short story using given clues | |
| | 10. *Rainforest* | • Completing sentences<br>• Reference to context<br>• Inferential and extrapolative questions | • Collective nouns<br>• Word associations | | | | | | • Creating an information chart to display in class |
| | 11. Peter and the Wolf | • Gap filling<br>• Factual, inferential, and extrapolative questions | • Suffixes<br>• Character adjectives | • Types of adverbs<br>• Conjunctions: *because* and *so* | • Spelling: words ending with *-er* and *-ar* | • Listening to a passage and stating true or false<br>• Dictation of a short passage | • Asking for and giving advice<br>• Enacting the play | • Creative writing based on the play | |
| Project 2 (DIY and bagless day activity) | | • Making an information chart | | | • Making a PowerPoint presentation | | | | |
| **VI. Outer Space** | 12. Kalpana Chawla | • MCQ<br>• Factual, inferential, and extrapolative questions | • Collocations | • Types of pronouns<br>• Main and auxiliary verbs | • Pronunciation: different sounds of *th*; words with *gh* sounds | • Listening to an interview and answering questions<br>• Dictation of a short passage | • Expressing agreement or disagreement | • Narrationg an incident | |
| | 13. *The Big Beyond* | • Completing sentences<br>• Reference to context<br>• Inferential and extrapolative questions | • Movement words<br>• Space-related phrases | | | | | | • Writing an anecdote |
| **VII. Different but Same** | 14. Earrings for Nina | • True and False<br>• Factual, inferential, and extrapolative questions | • Anagrams | • Order of adjectives<br>• Adjectives: degrees of comparison<br>• Apostrophe for contractions<br>• Apostrophe to show possession | • Pronunciation: soft and hard c sounds | • Listening to a passage and sequencing | • Speaking on a given topic using degrees of comparison | • Describing an event | |
| | 15. *I See What You Miss* | • Reference to context<br>• Factual, inferential, and extrapolative questions | • Words related to the senses | | | | | | • Writing a poem |
| **VIII. Humour** | 16. Lion on the Loose | • MCQ<br>• Factual, inferential, and extrapolative questions | • Crossword<br>• Phrasal verbs | • Simple future tense<br>• Types of sentences | • Spelling: words ending with *-sion, -cian, -tion* | • Listening to announcements and gap filling | • Talking about a book | • Writing a dialogue | |
| Project 3 (Bagless day activity) | | • Making a presentation on travelling to outer space | | | | • Making a scrapbook | | | |

# Contents

# Self-Assessment

**A. Fill in the blanks with the correct phrasal verbs.** (5 × 1)

call off | cheer up | find out | keep up | put on

1. We had to run to ______________ with them.
2. ______________! It is okay if you lose the game.
3. She tried to ______________ the name of the shop.
4. The young boy ______________ his clothes on his own.
5. The school had to ______________ the picnic because of rain.

**B. Fill in the blanks with the correct words given in brackets.** (10 × 0.5)

1. I have __________ this __________ already. (seen/scene)
2. Sam __________ his bike on the new __________. (rode/road)
3. The wind __________ away my __________ umbrella. (blue/blew)
4. My mother told me the __________ of a dragon with a long __________. (tail/tale)
5. The lion with the huge __________ is the __________ attraction of the zoo. (main/mane)

**C. Circle the correct words in the sentences.** (5 × 1)

1. This is our/ours house.
2. This is not my bag, it is her/hers.
3. Can you show my/mine friend the way?
4. My book is lost. Can I borrow your/yours?
5. The astronauts prepared for their/theirs first spacewalk.

**D. Fill in the blanks with the correct forms of the verbs.** (5 × 1)

1. The army ______________ (win) the battle.
2. My mother always ______________ (tell) me stories at night.
3. The lions ______________ (come) towards us. What do we do?
4. Don't ______________ (run) on the wet floor because it is slippery.
5. They ______________ (stand) near the door when I returned last night.

**E. Sort the countable and uncountable nouns into the correct boxes.** (10 × 0.5)

apple blood book sand man oil seat computer sugar water

| Countable | Uncountable |
|---|---|
| | |
| | |
| | |
| | |
| | |

**F. Look at the picture. Then, fill in the blanks with the correct position words.** (5 × 1)

1. The frog is ____________ the pond.
2. The bird is flying ____________ the park.
3. The butterfly is ____________ the children.
4. The children are sitting ____________ the slide.
5. The girl with the skipping rope is ____________ the grass.

*The answers are given on page 152.*

**Assessment**

1. If you score 4 or more in each section, you are ready to start the new chapters.
2. If you score less than 3 in section A, revise 'Phrasal Verbs'.
3. If you score less than 3 in section B, revise 'Homophones'.
4. If you score less than 3 in section C, revise 'Pronouns'.
5. If you score less than 3 in section D, revise 'Different Tenses of Verbs'.
6. If you score less than 3 in section E, revise 'Countable and Uncountable Nouns'.
7. If you score less than 3 in section F, revise 'Position Words'.

UNIT I

# Imagination

## Warm-up

**A. Work in pairs. Look at these pictures and try to identify these imaginary creatures. Do you know what special powers these animals are supposed to have?**

1. ________________

2. ________________

3. ________________

4. ________________

5. ________________

6. ________________

**B. Imagine and draw a fantastical beast. Does it look like a real animal? How is it different from that animal? Does it have any special powers? Share with your class.**

1 fantasy

# A Different Kind of Dragon

Cheryl Rao

## Curricular Goals

- develop a comprehensive range of vocabulary in various contexts
- develop fluency in reading and the ability to read with comprehension
- sustain effective communication skills for day-to-day interactions
- develop the ability to express themselves in writing

→

## Competencies

- can identify homonyms, words related to nature, and commonly misspelt words
- can understand different types of nouns and different tenses of verbs
- can give, accept, and refuse an invitation and write a thank-you note

## Reading

**a** *Do you believe in monsters? Long ago, the people of Brno, a city in Europe, were troubled by a water monster. Read the story to find out what happened when one of the fishermen decided to deal with it.*

Long ago, a horrible monster lived in the **swamps** between the two rivers that meet at Brno (Rivers Svitava and Svratka). No one had ever seen this monster. But the people knew it was there because many of those who entered the **marshes** or even went down to the river sometimes never came back. Their bodies were never found, and their families never knew what had happened to them.

Sometimes, late at night, people who passed by the swamp as they hurried home heard a **dreadful** roaring sound—and they went even faster because they feared that the monster would grab them and **crunch** their bones in seconds.

Since no one had seen the monster and **survived**, no one knew what kind of monster it was. So, they called it a **dragon**. But it was probably a different kind of

swamps: areas of extremely wet land with wild plants growing in it

marshes: very wet and muddy areas of land

dreadful: very bad and unpleasant

crunch: to crush something noisily between the teeth or under the feet

survived: remained alive

dragon: a fierce animal like a big lizard in legends and stories; it has wings and claws, and breathes out fire dragon because it was not known to fly, and it did not breathe fire and it did not **stray** very far from the water. 'All we have to do is keep away from the rivers and we'll be safe,' they said among themselves.

'That is true. But we need the water from the rivers. We cannot live without it.'

So, they kept going down to the water. And they kept losing their lives. The monster would suddenly **dart** out and **grab unsuspecting** people or it would **pounce** on animals that strayed to the rivers.

The monster **terrorized** the people for many years. No one was safe in Brno. 'We have to get rid of[1] the dragon,' said the **mayor** of the town. 'Whoever kills the dragon and brings its body to me will get a bag of gold coins.'

**Common idioms and proverbs**

1. **get rid of:** to make ourselves free of somebody or something that we don't want

For a long time, no one **volunteered**. Then, at last, a fisherman, who had not been able to work close to home for years for fear of the monster, said that he would get rid of the monster. He had grown tired of having to row far away from town to safer places – and also places where there were fish left (because the monster ate everything it found, and it seemed to like fish a lot). He had also grown tired of **mooring** his boat in a safe place far from town and far from his small hut.

The fisherman didn't tell anyone how he would do it, but he thought of something. He loaded his boat with the **carcass** of a goat and a bucket of caustic lime. 'What are you doing?' cried his wife when he told her where he was going. 'The monster will get you!'

**Cross-curricular Corner**

Caustic lime or calcium hydroxide is a chemical. It is used in industries to melt things and for cleaning.

'I have a plan,' said the fisherman. 'The monster will surely smell the blood of the goat and it will come to my boat…'

'What?' wailed his wife. 'And you think you can fight it **single-handedly** – with that bucket as a **weapon**?'

stray: (here) wander away
dart: to move suddenly and quickly
grab: to take hold of something suddenly and roughly
unsuspecting: unaware that something is going to happen
pounce: to leap on something and grab it
terrorized: kept somebody in a state of fear
mayor: the person who is elected to represent the city for a fixed period of time, and to run its government
volunteered: offered to do something without expecting any reward
mooring: (here) tying the boat to the land with a rope or chain
carcass: the body of a dead animal
single-handedly: without help from anyone else
weapon: an object used to kill or hurt others

'The bucket is the **key**,' replied the fisherman. 'When the monster opens its mouth and grabs the goat, I will throw the bucket of caustic lime in as well – and its insides will soon burn up and **dissolve**.'

'Why can't you fill the goat with caustic lime and leave it on the river bank? Why do you have to go there?'

'I don't know how long the monster will take to attack. If the caustic lime is in the goat, there'll soon be nothing left of the goat … I have to take this risk, or I will never be able to fish in these rivers again.'

Who helped the fisherman?

## Common idioms and phrases

2. **look sharp:** to ask someone to hurry up

'Then I will come with you!' declared his wife.

The fisherman **protested** but his wife would not listen to him. She got into the boat and would not move. At last, tired of arguing, the two of them set out in the boat. 'Look sharp[2],' whispered the fisherman.

'Believe me, I am,' his wife whispered back – and then, suddenly, both of them saw something long **streaking** towards them under the water.

What did the fisherman throw into the mouth of the monster?

'It's coming!' said the fisherman. He **edged** the carcass of the goat halfway over the **rim** of the boat so that the monster would have to open its mouth wide to grab it and drag it away. Then he got ready with the bucket.

Meanwhile, his wife, who could not allow her husband to do this alone, lifted up the **sturdy oar** in her hands and waited. She was ready to give the monster a hard hit on its head if everything her husband had planned didn't work!

But luckily, it did. The monster came towards the boat with its huge jaws wide open. Before it could grab the part of the goat that was **trailing** in the water, the fisherman threw the

key: (here) the most important thing
dissolve: (here) to melt
protested: (here) objected to; disagreed
streaking: (here) moving very quickly
edged: (here) pushed
rim: the edge of something
sturdy: strong and firm
oar: wooden pole with a flat end used for rowing a boat
trailing: dragging along slowly

contents of the bucket directly into the **gaping** mouth. The monster **clamped** its jaws shut and **jerked** away but it had caught a part of the goat.

The boat rocked crazily as the goat was dragged **overboard**. The fisherman and his wife held on for dear life[3]. They hoped that the monster would feel the effects of the caustic lime before it came up once more and **overturned** the boat.

### Common idioms and phrases

**3. hold on for dear life:** to hold somebody or something very tightly because of fear

**Frantically**, with strength they didn't even know they had, they rowed towards the shore. They paid no attention to the wild **thrashing** that was taking place in the water as they sped away. When they climbed out of the boat at last, they ran to high ground and then looked down at the water. A huge, long shape was floating by lifeless.

'It worked! It worked!' cried the fisherman. 'We killed the monster!'

The two of them screamed and jumped and cried **triumphantly** and people from Brno began to come to the riverside to see why they were making such a noise. When the others saw the huge body floating away, they grabbed **rakes** and sticks and tried to catch it and bring it to the shore to see what kind of dragon it was.

They dragged out a huge dead crocodile. And of course, the brave fisherman and his wife got their bag of gold coins. More importantly, the people of Brno were now free to go down to the rivers whenever they wanted.

gaping: wide open
clamped: (here) closed tightly
jerked: moved suddenly
overboard: over the side of a boat into the water
overturned: turned upside down; toppled
frantically: in a wild and uncontrolled way
thrashing: (here) the act of beating and lashing in the water
triumphantly: extremely happy because of succeeding in a task
rakes: garden tools with a row of metal teeth fixed to a long handle

### In a Nutshell

| | |
|---|---|
| **Who** | A fisherman and his wife |
| **What** | They killed a river monster. |
| **Where** | Brno, a city in Europe |
| **Why** | The monster killed the people and animals. |

### About the author

Cheryl Rao is a children's writer. She writes about travel, animals, adventures, and strange happenings for children of all ages.

## Comprehension

**A. Answer these questions.**

1. Why were the people of Brno afraid?
2. What happened to the people who went to the river?
3. What was different about the dragon?
4. What did the fisherman take with him to the river?
5. How did the fisherman succeed?

**B. Complete the flow chart to show the order of events in the story.**

1 The people of Brno were terrified because ____________________ ____________________ near the rivers Svitava and Svratka.

2 The people had never ____________________, but they imagined it to be ____________________.

3 The terrible monster caught ____________________ ____________________.

4 The people decided to ____________________ ____________________.

5 One day, the mayor announced ____________________ ____________________.

6 Nobody volunteered for a long time, but one day, a fisherman ____________________ ____________________.

7 The fisherman carried the ____________________ with him to kill the dragon. His wife went along with him.

8 They rowed out into the water and waited. Suddenly, they saw a ________
____________________________________________.

9 The fisherman's wife ____________________________________________,
while the fisherman edged the carcass ____________________________.

10 The monster came close and opened ______________________________,
and the fisherman poured ______________________________________.

11 The fisherman and his wife rowed quickly to the shore and shouted, 'We killed the monster!' The people came to see the monster's carcass ______________________________. It was a huge crocodile!

## Life Skills and Values

being brave and helpful

21ST CENTURY Critical Thinking

1. The fisherman decided to get rid of the dragon himself. Do you think his actions were brave?
2. The fisherman's wife insisted on going with him to kill the monster. Have you ever helped anyone in need? How?

## Vocabulary

homonyms

Read this sentence.

All we have to do is keep away from the rivers and we'll be **safe**.

Here, the word *safe* means 'without harm or danger'.

But *safe* can also mean 'a metal cupboard with locks, to keep money or something valuable'. It is a homonym.

**Homonyms** are words that have the same pronunciation and the same spelling but different meanings.

**A. Underline the homonyms in each pair of sentences. Then, match the meaning with the homonym.**

1. The thieves stole a lot of money from the bank. [a.]
   The old man sat on a bench near the bank of the river. [b.]
   a. a place to store money b. the land along a body of water

2. The bark of this tree can be used as medicine. [ ]
   The repeated barks of our dog woke us up last night. [ ]
   a. the sharp cry of a dog or a fox b. the tough outer covering of a tree

3. The man lifted the fallen tree with a crane and cleared the road. [ ]
   Every winter, you can see the cranes flying around the bird sanctuary. [ ]
   a. large, tall birds b. a large machine that lifts objects

4. I had to pay a fine because I did not return my library book on time. [ ]
   It was easy to build sandcastles with the fine sand at the beach. [ ]
   a. having very small grains b. money paid for breaking a rule

5. The football match was cancelled due to the sudden rain. [ ]
   Please give me a match to light the candle. [ ]
   a. a game or contest b. a thin piece of wood used to light a fire

words related to nature

ia **B. Read the clues and solve the crossword. You can take the help of a dictionary.**

**Across**

3. a small narrow river
4. the ground at the bottom of a sea or river

**Down**

1. a large body of fresh water that flows in a particular direction
2. a large water body surrounded by land on all sides
3. an area of wet land with wild plants growing in it
4. the edge of a river

**Grammar**

types of nouns

There are different types of nouns.

**Common nouns** are the general names of a person, place, or thing.

**Examples:** The **people** went to the **river** to fetch **water**.

**Proper nouns** are the special names given to a person, place, or thing.

**Examples:** **Brno** was a little town that had two rivers flowing near it, **Svitava** and **Svratka**.

**Collective nouns** are the names given to a group of people, animals, or things.

**Example:** A **flock** of goats lived near the fisherman's house.

**A. Underline the common nouns and circle the proper nouns.**

1. Diwali is an Indian festival.
2. India is my favourite country.
3. Australia is the land of kangaroos.
4. Our friends are going to Mexico in April.
5. The children are visiting the Big Temple in Thanjavur.

**B. Circle the correct collective nouns in the sentences.**

1. A herd/pack of dogs chased the man.
2. She bought a bunch/bouquet of bananas.
3. The school/team of fish swam across the ocean.
4. I saw a crew/litter of puppies jumping playfully near the beach.
5. A bunch/troop of monkeys come to the temple every morning.

material nouns

Read this sentence.

They went in his **boat**.

Here, *boat* is a thing we can see and touch. Such things are called **material nouns**.

**C. Fill in the blanks with the correct material nouns from the box.**

| steel | silver | cotton | leather | plastic | milk |
|---|---|---|---|---|---|

1. ____________ is harmful for the environment.
2. Curd, cheese, and *kheer* are made from ____________.
3. Rina has bought a pair of shoes made of ____________.
4. Sunita is wearing a beautiful bangle made of ____________.
5. All the water pipes in this house are made of ____________.
6. We should only wear clothes made of ____________ in summer.

## simple present tense

Read these sentences.

That **is** true. We **need** the water from the rivers.

The verbs *is* and *need* are in the simple present tense.

The **simple present tense** is used to state facts and talk about an action that takes place in the present moment and about things that happen regularly.

**D. Fill in the blanks with the simple present tense of the given verbs.**

1. The sun __rises__ (rise) in the east.
2. My mother ________ (work) in a bank.
3. Akshay's brother ________ (exercise) every day.
4. Rohan always ________ (complete) his homework on time.
5. Sharda ________ (help) her mother clean the house on weekends.
6. Many birds ________ (fly) south during winters, in search of warmer climates.

## present continuous tense

Read these sentences.

The dragon **is coming**.

A huge, long shape **is floating** by.

The verbs *is coming* and *is floating* are in the present continuous tense.

The **present continuous tense** tells us about an action that is going on at the time of speaking.

## ia E. Fill in the blanks with the present continuous tense of the given verbs.

1. Arya ___is reading___ (read) a book now.
2. Riya's cat ______________ (drink) milk from the saucer.
3. The naughty boys ______________ (climb) the mango tree.
4. My friends ______________ (watch) a football match on TV.
5. Jaya and her brother ______________ (leave) for home now.
6. Rustom ______________ (dig) the flower bed to plant the saplings.

## Study Skills

### Spelling

commonly misspelt words

**Underline the misspelt words. Correct the spellings and rewrite the sentences in your notebook. There may be more than one error in each sentence.**

1. The food in this restruant is better than the one down the road.
2. It is allmost 11 p.m. Usualy taxis are hard to find so late at night.
3. I wanted to give my parents a suprise gift.
4. You should beleive in yourself, in every situation.
5. Where is the calender? I want to see if I am free next Wensday.
6. Have you writen down evrything I said?

## Listening

listening for facts

**Listen to a passage about the mystery of the missing ice cream. Number the sentences in the order of events.**

- ☐ Radha was scared as there was no one else at home.
- ☐ Radha heard the doorbell and went to see who had come.
- ☐ Then she saw the cat running out of the kitchen.
- ☐ The cat came into the kitchen and ate all the ice cream.
- ☐ When Radha came back, the bowl was empty.
- ☐ She now knew who had eaten the ice cream.
- ☐ Radha sat down at the kitchen table with a bowl of ice cream.

## Speaking

giving, accepting, and refusing an invitation

**Meena's school is organizing their annual concert at 4 p.m. on Saturday. She wants to invite her friend, Tina. In pairs, enact the two conversations.**

**Meena:** Hi Tina! We have our annual school concert this Saturday. It would be great if you could attend.

**Tina:** Thank you, Meena. I would love to come. At what time does it start? **(accepting)** **OR,**

**Tina:** Thank you for inviting me, Meena. But I don't think I will be able to come. I am visiting my grandparents on Saturday. **(refusing)**

**Now, imagine your parents are taking you to an amusement park on Sunday. You can invite one of your friends to join you. Enact the conversation with your partner, taking turns to accept or refuse the invitation. Remember to give a reason for refusing the invitation. Use simple present tense or present continuous tense in your sentences.**

## Writing

writing a thank-you note

**Imagine that you live in Brno. Write a thank-you note to the fisherman and his wife for killing the dragon and making the town a safe place to live in.**

## Explore More

**Read** the story *Li Chi Slays the Serpent*. It is about a brave teenager who kills a snake that terrorizes the villagers.

**Watch** the film *Raya and the Last Dragon*. It is about a young girl who finds the last dragon to help save her village from monsters.

2 poem

# Oliphaunt

J. R. R. Tolkien

### Curricular Goals

- develop a comprehensive range of vocabulary in various contexts
- develop the ability to express themselves in writing

### Competencies

- can understand rhyming and sound words
- can write a notice

## Reading

**a** *Do you believe in magical creatures? Read this poem about* ***Oliphaunt****, which is one such magnificent magical creature found in Middle-earth, an imaginary place.*

Grey as a mouse,
Big as a house[1],
Nose like a snake,
I make the earth shake,
As I **tramp** through the grass;
Trees crack[2] as I pass.
With **horns** in my mouth
I walk in the South,
**Flapping** big ears.
Beyond count of years
I **stump** round and round,
Never lie on the ground,
Not even to die.
Oliphaunt am I,
Biggest of all,
Huge, old, and tall.

### Literary terms

1. This is an example of **simile**, where Oliphaunt is being compared to a big house.
2. This is an example of **onomatopoeia**. When something breaks, it makes a 'crack' sound.

Oliphaunt: an imaginary elephant-like creature with four tusks
tramp: to walk slowly with heavy steps
horns: (here) the four tusks
flapping: (here) moving the ears quickly from side to side
stump: to walk with heavy steps

If ever you'd meet me
You wouldn't forget me.
If you never do,
You won't think I'm true;
But old Oliphaunt am I,
And I never lie.

## In a Nutshell

**Who** Oliphaunt, a huge elephant-like creature

**What** Unforgettable

**Why** Trees break and the Earth shakes when Oliphaunt walks.

**Where** In the South (of Middle-earth)

## About the poet

John Ronald Reuel Tolkien, popularly known as J.R.R. Tolkien (1892–1973), is best known for *The Hobbit* and *The Lord of the Rings*. He created the imaginary world of Middle-earth. The poem *Oliphaunt* is an excerpt from *The Lord of the Rings*.

## Understanding the Poem

ia **A. Choose the correct options.**

1. How big is Oliphaunt?
   a. It is as big as the Earth. ☐
   b. It is as big as a house. ☐
   c. It is as big as a mouse. ☐
2. What happens when Oliphaunt walks?
   a. The other animals run towards him. ☐
   b. The houses break. ☐
   c. The Earth shakes. ☐

**B. Read the lines and answer the questions.**

1. *Biggest of all,*
   *Huge, old, and tall.*
   a. Who is the 'biggest of all'?
   b. What are the three ways in which we can describe it?
   c. In what ways does this creature resemble an elephant?

2. *If you never do,*
   *You won't think I'm true;*
   a. Who is the speaker?
   b. What does 'do' refer to?
   c. Why wouldn't we think the speaker is true?

## Life Skills and Values

imagination

1. Do you think Oliphaunt is a gentle creature despite its size?
2. Do you think a creature like Oliphaunt could ever exist? Why?

## Vocabulary

rhyming words

Look at these lines.

Grey as a **mouse**,

Big as a **house**,

The words *mouse* and *house* rhyme with each other, creating a rhythm.

**A. Make a list of the other rhyming words in the poem.**

**B. Write three rhyming words for each of the given words in your notebook.**

1. tap 2. round 3. shoe 4. gate 5. break 6. red

sound words

In the poem, trees **crack** when Oliphaunt walks past them. The word *crack* is a sound word or onomatopoeia. It is similar to the sound of something breaking.

**C. Read the sentences and underline the sound words.**

1. The boy splashed around in the pool.
2. The honking of the car startled the baby.
3. The chirping of the birds filled the forest.
4. The coconut hit the ground with a thump.
5. I could hear the pitter-patter of the rain outside.
6. The door of the old house creaked as Ria opened it.

## Activity

dumb charades

**A. Work in pairs and choose any one of the given feeling words. Write two actions related to the feeling word you have chosen. One is done for you.**

1. **happy:** *seeing my dog after school; having an ice cream*

2. **unhappy** 3. **angry** 4. **scared** 5. **shy**

**Now, each pair will act out the actions they have noted down before the class, without using any words. The rest of the class will guess the situation.**

writing a notice

**B. Notices give information about various events. Read this notice.**

**Marigold School, Siliguri**
**NOTICE**

1 December

**Clean-up Drive**

The school is organising a clean-up drive on 10 December.
All members of the school's Green Environment Club are requested to be present for a meeting on 5 December at 11:00 a.m. to discuss the details of the drive and plan the events for the day.

Sasha Duggal
*(President, Green Environment Club)*

**Now, write a notice inviting students of your school to take part in a fancy dress competition being organized on Children's Day. The theme is 'magical creatures'. There would be prizes for the best-dressed participants.**

## Explore More

**Read** *Fantastic Beasts and Where to Find Them*. This interesting book by J.K. Rowling talks about many interesting magical creatures.

**Watch** the film series *How to Train Your Dragon*. Follow the adventures of a young boy, Hiccup, and his dragon, Toothless.

**Listen** to *Neon Pegasus*. This cheerful song by Parry Gripp is about a magical creature.

UNIT II

# Our Country

## Warm-up

**A. Here are some activities you can do while visiting different parts of India. Match them with the places given in the box.**

INDIA FOCUS

| | |
|---|---|
| Ahmedabad, Gujarat | Gulmarg, Kashmir |
| Kovalam, Kerala | Manali, Himachal Pradesh |

1. rafting

2. surfing

3. snowball fighting

4. kite flying

**B. Now, working in pairs, tell your friend which of these places you would like to visit and why.**

21ST CENTURY Critical Thinking

**C. Solve the crossword.**

**Across:**

5. a low stretch of land between hills, especially one that has a river flowing through it
6. a long narrow piece of land which sticks out from a larger piece of land and is surrounded by water on three sides
7. an area of wet, muddy, or marshy land with wild plants growing in it
9. a hill of sand near the sea or in a desert
10. an area of land or stones beside the sea

**Down:**

1. a large area of high and fairly flat land
2. an area of land that is higher than the land that surrounds it, but smaller than a mountain
3. a long, narrow valley with very steep sides
4. a very tall or high area of land with a peak at the top, and steep sides
8. a long, narrow channel under the sea or cut into the ground

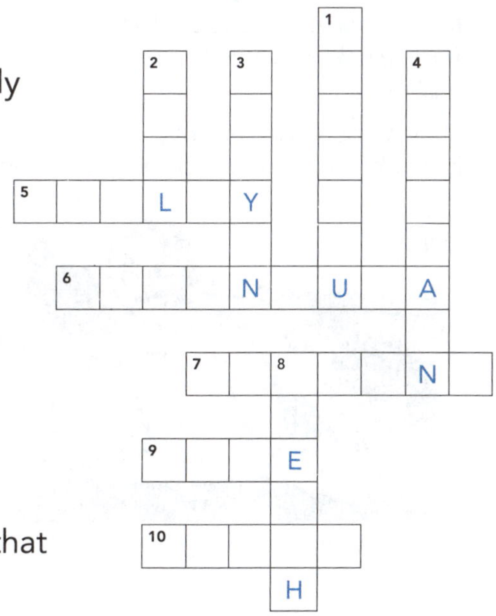

epistolary story

# 3 North, South, East, West

C. G. Salamander

### Curricular Goals

- develop a comprehensive range of vocabulary in various contexts
- develop fluency in reading and the ability to read with comprehension
- sustain effective communication skills for day-to-day interactions
- develop the ability to express themselves in writing

### Competencies

- can understand the uses of different prefixes and suffixes
- can identify different types of adjectives, the subject and predicate in a sentence, and words of Indian origin
- can participate in a group discussion and write an informal letter

## Reading

**a** *In 2023, Shaana travelled the length and breadth of our country with her parents. She explored the many landscapes of India. She documented her travels in letters that she wrote to her friends back at school in the Andaman Islands. Read this* ***epistolary*** *story to find out more about Shaana's travels and our country.*

July 26, 2023

Dear Class 4B,

Miss Priya must have told you that I won't be coming to school for the next five months. I'm travelling across India with Amma and Appa.

They will teach me history, geography, science, and maths. I will be back next year. I miss you all and hope you miss me too.

Love,
Shaana

Who will teach Shaana for the next five months?

epistolary: a story that is written as a series of letters

July 30, 2023

Hi everyone,

You won't believe where I am!

I'm way up in the north, near the Thajiwas **glacier** in Kashmir. The glacier is white and blue, and we have to wear four layers of warm clothes. Appa and Amma love it here, and they like throwing snowballs at each other.

I also like the snow, but my hands are shaking from not wearing gloves, so I don't think I can write any more.

Send my love to our class teacher.

Love,
Shaana

August 17, 2023

Dear class,

We took a bus to Jammu yesterday and then a train to reach our **cabin** in Himachal Pradesh. It is very quiet, and we can see many mountains from our cabin. Colourful birds wake me with their chirping when the sun rises in the east.

I also think I hear bears growling in the west when it gets dark. But Amma says that's just Appa **snoring**. I would love to meet a bear and give it a hug.

With love from your best friend,
Shaana

August 27, 2023

Hi everyone,

Did you know that Arunachal Pradesh is far away from Himachal Pradesh? Himachal is in the north, but Arunachal is all the way in the east. I thought all the Pradesh states were next to each other.

We had to change two trains and drive a long way to reach here. This morning, we walked through a forest to reach our **treehouse**. The forest here is so thick that if you **blink** or stop to tie your shoelaces, you will get lost.

I love Arunachal the best so far and am beginning to enjoy myself. I hope to see **red pandas**.

With love,
Shaana

Where does Shaana see the treehouse?

glacier: a large mass of ice that moves slowly

cabin: a small, simple house made of wood, usually found in the mountains

snoring: breathing in a very noisy way while sleeping

treehouse: a small house-like structure built among the branches of a tree

blink: to shut your eyes and open them again quickly

red pandas: rare bear-like animals that live in bamboo forests in the Himalayas

September 6, 2023

Dear classmates,

It did not take any time at all to travel southwest and get to the Sundarbans in West Bengal. Today, Amma and Appa took me out onto the river in a small boat. Amma tells me that places like the Sundarbans are called **wetlands**. I never knew such a place existed, and that it was possible for trees called **mangroves** to grow in seawater! But Amma is sad about how much this place floods today.

We also saw crocodiles and a lonely snake while boating.

I hope they don't follow us home.

How is everyone? Are you missing me yet?

Love,
Shaana

September 29, 2023

Hi everyone,

We travelled across the country, all the way from east to west, from West Bengal to Rajasthan, and it took us two and a half days by train!

I don't know why my Amma and Appa brought me to the middle of the desert. It is hot, dry, and there's sand everywhere. It is like a beach without the sea! But I do really love the clothes people wear here. They're so pretty and colourful.

I am sure you are all studying hard for your half-yearly exams. Amma gave me a test today, and I passed with 88 per cent.

Love,
Shaana

October 4, 2023

Dear class,

Today was the best day ever! We drove south from the desert to the Narmada River. It flows all the way from the centre of India to the Arabian Sea. It took us half a day to reach there. In the afternoon, Amma, Appa, and I went **rafting** in the river, and you won't believe how wild and scary it was.

I always thought rivers were calm, but up close they are very fast. Appa says that there used to be more water, and rafting was much scarier then.

We were fully wet by the time we were done. Appa was so scared that he swore never to go rafting ever again. I love the water so much and can't wait to go back.

Your best friend,
Shaana

wetlands: areas of land that have marshes or swamps

mangroves: tropical trees found near water with twisted roots that grow above the ground

rafting: the sport or pastime of travelling down a river in a rubber or inflatable raft

October 12, 2023

Dear classmates,

Amma and Appa are fast asleep, and I should be sleeping too, but I just love looking out the window. I think we're in the southwestern part of the country, in Goa, and you won't believe how nice the **plateaus** look. There are so many hills here, and beaches too.

There are also a lot of tunnels that the train goes through. I used to be afraid of tunnels, but I'm not anymore. Someday, I wish we could all go on a tour of the plateaus. Maybe when we're older.

Love,
Shaana

November 1, 2023

Dear friends,

We travelled south and our trip will end soon. We reached Chennai a few days ago.

On the way to Puducherry, we decided to learn how to **surf**.

I think I'm good at it now because I only fell off my **surfboard** twice.

Amma and Appa splashed water on each other and behaved like children. It's a good thing I was there to control them.

The beaches here are not like the ones we have on our island. The waves are a lot rougher, and the water is browner, but I still like it here.

Love,
Shaana

plateaus: areas of high and fairly flat ground

surf: a sport where one stands or lies on a surfboard and rides on a wave

surfboard: a long narrow board that is used for surfing

November 21, 2023

Hi everyone,

I just crossed the Pamban Bridge. I could see the ocean on both sides. How amazing that a train can travel across the sea like this!

I'm almost home, and I can't wait to give you my final letter in person.

Love,
Shaana

November 23, 2023

*Dear classmates,*

*I thought Amma and Appa would be tired from all our travelling, but we made one last stop at the Olaikaadu beach before we reached home. And I'm so happy we did.*

*Amma wanted to teach me how to* ***dive****, but they did not have diving suits my size, so I spent the day floating and looking at the fish while my parents dove below me.*

*We found all sorts of pebbles on the beach, and I can't wait to give them to you in person soon.*

*Your best friend,*
*Shaana*

What was special about the Pamban Bridge?

December 1, 2023

Dear Amma and Appa,

I can't believe we travelled across the whole country! I know we're going to miss visiting the forests, glaciers, deserts, wetlands, plateaus, and mountains. And we are going to miss hearing all those new languages and meeting all those different people. But we're finally home now, and we can join our friends again.

I hope we get to travel like this again, and maybe next time we can take our friends with us.

With love,
Shaana

dive: to jump into water with your head and arms going in first

## In a Nutshell

**Who** Shaana, a young girl

**When** Five months in the year 2023

**What** She travelled throughout India with her parents and sent letters to her friends back in the Andaman Islands.

## About the author

C. G. Salamander is a writer, comic journalist, and editor who has been published in India and abroad. He has written many books including *Puu*, *Arun in Ruins*, *Bounce*, and a series known as *House of Cloud*. He currently splits his time between Chennai and the Netherlands.

## Comprehension

### A. Choose the correct options.

1. Shaana did not attend school for ______________ months.
   a. four b. five c. six d. seven
2. Shaana visited the ______________ Glacier in Kashmir.
   a. Thajiwas b. Gangotri c. Himachal d. Jammu
3. Shaana hoped to see red pandas in ______________.
   a. Himachal Pradesh b. Kashmir c. Arunachal Pradesh d. Tamil Nadu
4. Shaana loved the pretty and colourful clothes in ______________.
   a. Kashmir b. Arunachal Pradesh c. Rajasthan d. Gujarat
5. Shaana learned to ______________ after they reached Olaikaadu Beach.
   a. dive b. surf c. climb d. swim

### B. We can understand the qualities of a person by looking at what he or she feels or does. Answer the following questions and find lines from the story to support your answers.

Critical Thinking

**Shaana**

1. Does Shaana like to share her experiences with her friends?
2. Does Shaana obey her parents and listen when they ask her to do something?
3. Was Shaana willing to admit that she was scared?
4. Was Shaana grateful/thankful?

**C. Answer these questions in a few lines.**

1. Why was Shaana not able to attend school for five months?
2. What did Shaana tell her classmates about Sundarbans?
3. How did Shaana describe her experience with river rafting?
4. What did Shaana see when she travelled to the southernmost tip of India?
5. What did Shaana tell her parents in the letter she wrote to them?

## Life Skills and Values

appreciating your country

1. Shaana had a wonderful time travelling across India. Do you think she enjoys/appreciates the beauty of the country? Pick out sentences from the text to support your answer.
2. What are the things that you think Shaana would have learnt travelling across India?

## Vocabulary

prefixes: *un-*, *dis-*, *re-*

**Prefixes** are letters that can be added to the beginning of words to form new words. They are often used to form opposites.

**Examples:** Shaana was **unable** to go to school. (*un-* + able = unable)
Shaana's parents **revisited** places. (*re-* + visit = revisit)

Look at these common prefixes.

**Prefixes**

| *un-* (not): unclean, unusual | *dis-* (not, opposite of): dissatisfied, disagree | *re-* (again): restart, rename |
|---|---|---|

**A. Rewrite the given words by adding *un-*, *dis-*, or *re-*.**

| | | | |
|---|---|---|---|
| 1. like | *unlike* | 4. act | ________ |
| 2. comfort | ________ | 5. appear | ________ |
| 3. fit | ________ | 6. create | ________ |

**B. Fill in the blanks with words formed by adding *un-*, *dis-*, or *re-* to the given words.**

1. Ratna ________ (likes) having eggs for breakfast.
2. Priya is ________ (happy) because she lost her favourite pen.

3. My mother has asked me to ________________ (heat) the leftover food.
4. The umpire is looking at the ________________ (play) before making his decision.
5. The children stared in ________________ (belief) as the magician made the rabbit vanish.
6. Rita's clothes and toys are scattered around the room. She is so ________________ (tidy).

adjectives with suffixes *-ing* and *-less*

Some adjectives are formed using **suffixes** such as *-ing* or *-less*. They are often used to form words that describe a person, thing, or place.

**Examples:** How **amazing** that a train can travel across the sea like this.
(amaze + *-ing* = amazing)
She was **careless**. (care + *-less* = careless)

Look at these common suffixes.

**Suffixes**

- *-ing* (with): amazing, interesting
- *-less* (without): careless, meaningless

ia **C. Rewrite the given words by adding *-ing* or *-less*. Some words may take both suffixes.**

| | | | |
|---|---|---|---|
| 1. help | helpless | 4. tire | ________________ |
| 2. care | ________________ | 5. fear | ________________ |
| 3. home | ________________ | 6. worry | ________________ |

## Grammar

types of adjectives

An **adjective** is a word that describes a person or thing. It gives extra information about them, such as their size, shape, colour, or a particular quality.

Read these lines.

The glaciers are **white** and **blue**, and we have to wear **four** layers of clothes.
We can see **many** mountains.

In these sentences, the words *white, blue, four,* and *many* help us to learn more about the *glaciers, layers of clothes,* and *mountains,* respectively. These describing words are called adjectives.

Some adjectives also tell us the number or position of people, animals, and things.

**Example:** We have to wear **four** layers of clothes.

Some adjectives do not show the exact number but tell us how much of something is there.

**Example:** We can see **many** mountains.

**Language Booster**

Adjectives usually appear *before* the nouns they describe. Adjectives can also be used with pronouns. They do not appear before pronouns.

**A. Read the paragraph and underline the adjectives.**

It was a hot afternoon in the quiet, dusty village of Sattenapalle in Andhra Pradesh. Sarvesh, all of ten years old, sat on a rectangular piece of rock under his favourite tree, waiting for his father. They were going to the big town nearby. The yellow sun shone brightly on the boy's face, and he saw many flowers near him. He counted five bees buzzing around the flowers. Ten minutes later, he heard his father's footsteps. He stood up excitedly and ran to his father.

**B. Fill in the blanks with the suitable adjectives.**

1. __________ fruits are in the boxes.
2. He could carry only __________ bags.
3. She bought a __________ vase from India.
4. The girl wrote a/an __________ book yesterday.
5. My sister saw __________ people outside our house last week.

## subject and predicate

You know that a sentence has two parts. The part of a sentence which tells us what it is about is the **subject**. The subject may be a noun, pronoun, or a group of words.

The part of a sentence which contains the verb tells us something about the subject. It is called the **predicate**.

**Examples:** **We** took another train yesterday.
**Amma, Appa, and I** were rafting in the river.

To find the subject of a sentence, ask the question *who?* or *what?* to the verb. In the first sentence, when we ask, 'Who took another train yesterday?', the answer is *We*. This is the subject. The rest of the sentence is the predicate.

In the second sentence, the subject is *Amma, Appa, and I,* while the predicate is *were rafting in the river.*

**C. Read the sentences. Circle the subjects and underline the predicates.**

1. I write letters to my friends.
2. My sister loves going to the beach.
3. The girls went to the mall together.
4. The boy is making a house with toy blocks.
5. Kathy is trying to get her cat down from the tree.
6. My mother and grandmother paint many pictures.

## Study Skills

### Dictionary Skills

words of Indian origin

**Look at the following entry for the word chutney in an online dictionary. It is an Indian word which is now used commonly in English.**

Definition of 'chutney'

Learner: chutney | Image | English: chutney | American: chutney | Example sentences | Trends

**chutney**
(tʃΔtni)

Word Frequency

**Collins** COBUILD

**Word forms:** plural **chutneys**

Variable noun

Chutney is a cold sauce made from fruit, vinegar, sugar, and spices. It is sold in jars and you eat it with meat or cheese.

*...mango chutney.*

**Use an online dictionary to find the meanings of these words of Indian origin.**

| | | | |
|---|---|---|---|
| 1. bungalow | 3. jute | 5. bazaar | 7. shampoo |
| 2. curry | 4. veranda | 6. cheetah | 8. pyjamas |

## Listening

listening for information

**Listen to a telephone conversation and complete the sentences. In it, a travel agent is telling someone about where to stay, and what to see and do when visiting the Rann Utsav in Kutch, Gujarat.**

1. The person is calling from ______________________.
2. The call is about the ______________________.
3. The Tent City is in ______________________.
4. Visitors can visit some ______________________ ______________________.
5. They can buy pieces of exquisite ______________________ ______________________.

## Speaking

group discussion

21ST CENTURY Collaboration

**There are many beautiful types of places in India: mountains, valleys, coasts, deserts, and plateaus. Given a choice, would you like to visit a hill station or a sea beach for a vacation? Form two groups and have a discussion on the topic: *Is a beach vacation better than one in the hills?***

You can use the following points.

| Group A: Hill Station | Group B: Sea Beach |
|---|---|
| • Cooler | • Sea breeze |
| • Lots of trees, different animals | • Sand, water, fish |
| • Hiking, trekking | • Surfing, swimming |

**Useful words and phrases**

- I feel that…
- I believe that…
- I agree with you, but…
- I do not agree with this point…

## Writing



Shaana writes many letters to her friends about her adventures while travelling. The letters that we write to our friends and family are called **informal letters**. These letters talk about how we feel or what we saw or did. We do not write informal letters to ask for permission. When we write an informal letter, we write about these:

- the date, for example, *10 September 2023*
- the place we are writing from, for example, *Shillong*
- a simple salutation, for example, *Dear Mom / Dear friends*
- the body of the letter consisting of an introduction, for example, *I am writing to tell you about my adventure …* followed by more details and a conclusion
- a sign off or an ending note, for example, *Yours lovingly* followed by name/Signature.

**A sample letter:**

*November 23, 2023* ← Date

Salutation → *Dear classmates,*

Introduction → *I thought Amma and Appa would be tired from all our travelling, but we made one last stop at the Olaikaadu beach before we reached home. And I'm so happy we did.*

*Amma wanted to teach me how to dive, but they did not have diving suits my size, so I spent the day floating and looking at the fish while my parents dove below me.* ← Body of the letter

Conclusion → *We found all sorts of pebbles on the beach, and I can't wait to give them to you in person tomorrow.*

End note → *Your best friend,*

*Shaana* ← Signature

**Shaana writes to her friends about every part of her journey. Think of a place in India that you have recently visited, such as the place your grandparents or your cousins live in. Compare it with your city and write a letter to your friend about your trip.**

**You can use the following points in your letter:**

- The place you visited
- The things you saw
- How the place was different from your hometown

## Explore More

**Read** *My Vacation*. This story by Ozi Okaro is about two siblings exploring different countries in Africa.

**Watch** the film *Peabody and Sherman*. It is about how a young boy learns history in real time, using a time machine.

**Listen** to *If You're Gonna Travel Far*, which is a song about travelling.

poem

# 4 Land of Glories

Rehana Ali

## Curricular Goals

- develop a comprehensive range of vocabulary in various contexts
- sustain effective communication skills for day-to-day interactions

## Competencies

- can understand word pairs and alliteration
- can recite a poem with correct stress

## Reading

**a** *India is a vast country with people who speak different languages, eat different kinds of food, and take part in many festivals. Read this poem which celebrates the richness of our country's culture.*

INDIA FOCUS

Nature's best gifts were **showered**
On this, our **wondrous** land
Where faith, friendship, **unity**,
And love go **hand in hand**.

**Lofty**, **snow-capped** mountains
That seem to touch the sky,
Rivers, lakes and oceans:
Such sights that greet the eye.

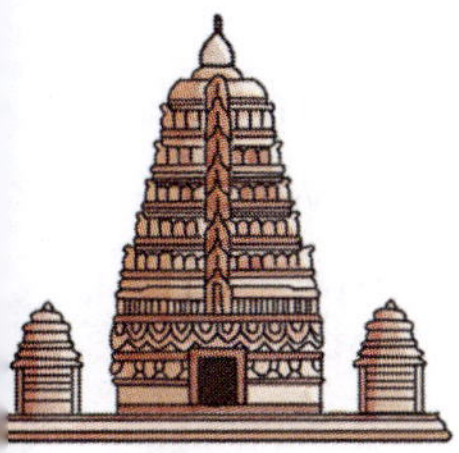

The forts, temples and palaces
That mark our history,
Sing **sagas**[1] of wise kings and queens,
Of their lives and **gallantry**.

The fearlessness of Lakshmibai,
The **deeds** of Ashoka the Great,
Stories of **heroism** and courage,
Have shaped our country's **fate**.

The Mughal gardens in Kashmir
Chittorgarh tower soaring high
The Taj Mahal in Agra
Are so pleasing to the eye.

### Literary term

1. This is an example of **alliteration**, where the letter *s* is repeated in consecutive words.

showered: gave somebody something in large quantities
wondrous: strange and beautiful
unity: when people or groups come together and work for a common purpose
hand in hand: together
lofty: very high
snow-capped: covered with snow on top
sagas: long stories about adventure or bravery
gallantry: bravery, especially in battle
deeds: actions
heroism: great courage
fate: (here) future

Our wildlife **thrives** in **sanctuaries**
In forests, safe and sound,
Their **pristine** beauty yet **untouched**,
Peace and harmony **abound**.

With years of **toil** and **struggle**
Our land's **prospered**, one can tell,
With education for our children
Jobs for the youth as well.

With the best of railways in the world,
Technology and science too,
Ours is a country that has grown with time,
To make our dreams come true.

### Cross-curricular Corner

Lakshmibai, the Queen of Jhansi, fought in India's first war of independence in 1857.

Ashoka was an Indian emperor who spread Buddhism to many parts of the world.

The Mughal gardens were built by various Mughal rulers in cities like Delhi, Agra, and Srinagar. They are also found in neighbouring countries which were part of the Mughal empire.

The Chittorgarh tower refers to a tall victory monument in Chittorgarh Fort in Rajasthan. It was built by Rana Kumbha, the king of Mewar.

thrives: grows well
sanctuaries: places where birds or animals live freely
pristine: pure
untouched: (here) not damaged
abound: are plentiful
toil: very hard or tiring work
struggle: a long and hard fight to get something
prospered: developed successfully

### In a Nutshell

**What** The natural beauty and man-made attractions

**Who** People of India

**Where** India

**How** The country has prospered after years of hard work and struggle.

### About the poet

Rehana Ali is a teacher who lives and teaches in Lucknow. She loves to write, and India is one of her favourite topics.

## Understanding the Poem

### A. Read the lines and answer the questions.

1. *Stories of heroism and courage*
   *Have shaped our country's fate.*
   a. Whose stories of 'heroism and courage' are being referred to?
   b. How have they shaped 'our country's fate'?
   c. Are these stories true?

2. *In forests safe and sound*
   *Their pristine beauty yet untouched...*
   a. Whose 'pristine beauty' is being talked about?
   b. What are the safe areas in the forests called?
   c. What is the meaning of the word 'untouched' in these lines?

## B. Answer these questions.

1. What are the things that go hand in hand in India?
2. What are the natural sights that greet the eye in India?
3. What do our forts, temples, and palaces sing of?
4. Name the three places of historical interest mentioned in the poem.
5. What are some of the things which show that our country has prospered?

## Life Skills and Values

appreciating our country

Critical Thinking

1. The poem talks about India's natural beauty, history, forests, and modern developments. Write down any two nouns from the poem which fall under each of these groups.
2. What do you think we can learn from our history?

## Vocabulary

word pairs

**Word pairs** are words that are commonly used together and joined by *and/or*. They always appear in the same order.

**Examples:** **safe and sound**, **peace and harmony**, **right or wrong**

## A. Fill in the blanks with the given words to complete the word pairs.

seek    low    socks    pepper    out    white

1. She searched high and __________ for her pencil box.
2. Could you pass me some salt and __________, please?
3. My father has been in and __________ of the garage all day.
4. Why don't you wear your black and __________ dress today?
5. The children are playing hide and __________ since morning.
6. Rima took off her wet shoes and __________, and kept them at the door.

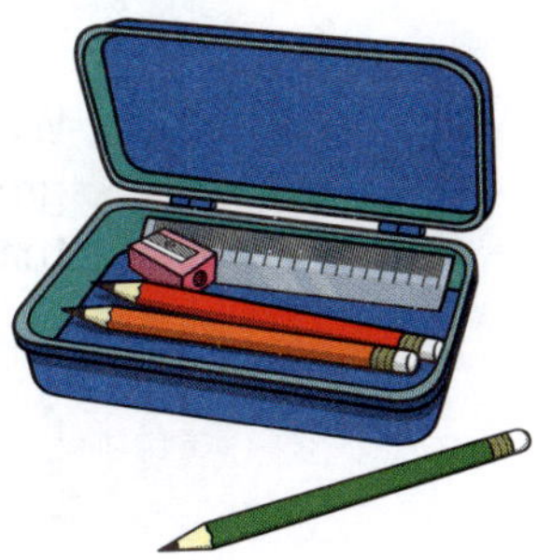

alliteration

Look at this line from the poem.

Sing sagas of wise kings and queens

The phrase *sing sagas* is an example of **alliteration**, as the letter s is repeated in words placed next to each other.

**B. Circle the words in these sentences that show alliteration.**

1. The lonely lion licked his lips hungrily.
2. Bobby bounced the ball in the backyard.
3. My sister happily helped me with my homework.
4. Polly the parrot always wanted a piece of my pizza.
5. The bunch of red roses was wrapped with a ribbon.

## Activity

reciting a poem with correct stress

**Listen to your teacher read the poem aloud. You will notice that some words are spoken with more stress than the others, in order to create a rhythm.**

**Now read these lines from the poem aloud, putting stress on the words in bold.**

**Nature's** best **gifts** were **showered**
On **this**, our **wondrous** land
Where **faith, friendship, unity,**
And **love** go **hand** in **hand**.

**Then, underline the stressed words in the next two stanzas of the poem, and recite them in class.**

## Explore More

**Read** the book *Rani Lakshmibai* by Sonia Mehta. It describes the life of the famous ruler of Jhansi who fought fiercely against the British.

**Watch** the Oscar-winning short film *The Elephant Whisperers*. It is about a group of people in India who take care of elephants. This shows the qualities that Indians are known for—love, affection, and respect for nature.

**Listen** to a popular Punjabi folk song, *Baajre Da Sitta*. It celebrates the simplicity, hard work, and togetherness of rural living, all set to a cheerful and lively tune.

UNIT III

# Adventure

## Warm-up

**A. What does going on an adventure mean to you? Circle the adventure words hidden in the word grid.**

21ST CENTURY Critical Thinking

| H | E | X | P | L | O | R | E | R | B |
|---|---|---|---|---|---|---|---|---|---|
| B | U | S | P | C | R | D | W | E | T |
| C | I | V | C | A | O | Z | T | T | H |
| D | A | N | G | E | R | P | X | T | R |
| R | O | U | T | D | O | O | R | J | I |
| I | D | A | R | I | N | G | I | O | L |
| S | F | X | Q | G | N | I | R | A | L |
| K | R | E | R | I | L | P | Z | E | W |
| G | P | E | Y | W | J | K | W | I | U |
| E | D | W | L | I | L | F | Y | C | G |

**B. You will read a story about the hero, Robin Hood, in this unit. Once, Robin's enemy, the Sheriff of Nottingham organised an archery contest. He hoped that Robin would come to take part in it and get captured. But Robin came in disguise, won the contest, and escaped. Now, fill in the dialogue in the following comic strip about the incident.**

graphic story 5

# The Hound in the Red Jersey

Edith Nesbit

### Curricular Goals

- develop a comprehensive range of vocabulary in various contexts
- develop fluency in reading and the ability to read with comprehension
- sustain effective communication skills for day-to-day interactions
- develop the ability to express themselves in writing

→

### Competencies

- can use similes correctly
- can understand different types of verbs and punctuations, and pronounce different words of *al* sounds
- can give a speech and make a diary entry

## Reading

**a** *This story is based on an extract from the book* The Railway Children, *about three children, Bobbie, Peter, and Phyllis Waterbury. They come to live in a country cottage near a railway station after their father is arrested wrongly for a crime. Read this story to find out how they are drawn into an adventure and help someone.*

*A game the local school boys play in the story. It is based on the concept of a hound or a hunting dog, chasing a hare. One boy, the Hare, went first, scattering pieces of torn paper after him. The others, the Hounds, followed him using the paper clues and tried to catch him before he came back to the school.

The next day, the children went to the railway line to see the paper chase. They carried a **hearty** lunch which Mother had packed for them.

Soon, the Hounds followed.

Where did the children go to see the paper chase?

By the time the children reached the top of the hill, they were **breathless**. They came down to a spot from where they could see the end of the tunnel.

The Hounds came soon after, in twos and threes, walking slowly.

They waited and waited, but the boy did not appear.

hearty: filling
breathless: not able to breathe easily

jersey: a knitted piece of clothing that covers the upper part of the body, like a sweater

Who did not come out from the tunnel?

## Cross-curricular Corner

Manholes were small openings cut into the walls of train tunnels. They were meant to be a shelter for workers if a train came by suddenly.

sickly: unhealthy and pale
dazzling: extremely bright
limply: having no strength or energy

The children tried to wake the boy up by splashing some milk which they had on his forehead, and rubbing his hands.

The boy felt much better after drinking milk. He tried to move, but then **groaned** in pain.

How did the children try to wake up the boy?

The three of them carried the boy to the nearest manhole. Then, Peter and Phyllis left to get help. Bobbie started to work on the boy's foot.

First, she took his boot off.

Then, she took off her **petticoat** and placed it under his foot.

Then she wet her handkerchief with milk and put it on the foot.

groaned: made a deep sound in pain
tripped: fell down hitting one's foot on something
beastly: unpleasant, terrible
petticoat: a thin skirt, worn under another skirt or dress

She wet the hanky again and placed it on his forehead.

Bobbie and the boy talked as they waited for help. Jim, as he was called, had no mother. His father lived far away.

Meanwhile, Peter and Phyllis had found help at the nearest farmhouse. They returned with farm men who carried Jim out in a **stretcher**.

Jim was carried in. He was pale from the pain.

Mother kissed him as if he had been Peter. The boy, looking at her kind eyes, felt a new rush of strength.

stretcher: a long piece of canvas with a pole along each side, used to carry a patient

lame: unable to walk well due to a foot injury

## In a Nutshell

**Who** Bobbie, Peter, Phyllis, and the boy in red jersey

**What** The boy is injured during a Hare and the Hounds race.

**Where** In a railway tunnel

**How** The children give him milk, mend his broken leg, and take him home.

### About the author

Edith Nesbit (1858–1924) was an English author and poet who wrote stories, mostly for children. Some of her notable works are *The Story of the Treasure Seekers*, *The Railway Children*, and *Five Children and It*.

## Comprehension

**A. Write whether the following statements are true (T) or false (F). Write the false statements correctly in your notebook.**

1. The children were excited because they were participating in a game.
2. The children climbed the hill so that they could see the end of the tunnel.
3. Peter noticed that the boy in the red jersey hadn't come out of the tunnel.
4. The boy in the red jersey had broken his arm.
5. The children splashed milk on the boy's forehead to wake him up.
6. Bobbie brought home a lame dog for her mother to look after.

**B. Answer these questions.**

1. Where did the three children go to see the paper chase?
2. Why did the children decide to go inside the tunnel?
3. What did the children do when they heard a train coming?
4. In what condition did they find Jim?
5. Where did the children go for help? Who helped them?
6. Where did the children take Jim? Why?

## Life Skills and Values

courage and quick thinking

21ST CENTURY Critical Thinking

1. Did the children do the right thing by going inside the tunnel to find Jim even though it was risky?
2. Do you think the children were intelligent in the way they handled the situation? Give reasons for your answer.

## Vocabulary

similes

You know that we can use a **simile** to compare two things, using the words *as* or *like*.

**Example:** Inside the tunnel, it was **as dark as the night**.

**A. Complete the following similes using the given words.**

bee  cucumber  bird  nails  snail  giraffe  coal  velvet

1. as tough as __________
2. as cool as a __________
3. as slow as a __________
4. as busy as a __________
5. as free as a __________
6. as tall as a __________
7. as soft as __________
8. as black as __________

**B. Underline the similes in these sentences and state the two things being compared.**

1. The wrestler was <u>as strong as an ox</u>.
   The wrestler is being compared to an ox.
2. The runner was as fast as a hare.
   __________ is being compared to __________.
3. Sam is as hungry as a bear. He has not eaten the whole day.
   __________ is being compared to __________.
4. Harry's broomstick was as light as a feather.
   __________ is being compared to __________.
5. The old village headman is as wise as an owl.
   __________ is being compared to __________.

regular and irregular verbs

Verbs that form past tense by adding *-ed* to themselves are **regular verbs**.

**Example:** The children **reached** the top of the hill.
reach + *ed* = reached

Verbs that change their form completely to form past tense are **irregular verbs**.

**Example:** The children **went** to the railway line.
go → went

**C. Underline the verbs in the sentences. Write whether they are regular or irregular.**

1. The queen <u>arrived</u> early. regular verb
2. She controlled her laughter. ____________
3. It was a beautiful Sunday morning. ____________
4. The villagers heard a strange sound. ____________
5. People travelled to the old woman's house. ____________
6. The boys played football during their summer vacation. ____________

## Grammar

transitive and intransitive verbs

Read these sentences.

They **found** the *boy* nearby.

He **was lying** against the wall.

In the first sentence, the word *boy* is the **object** of the verb *found*. It answers the question 'They found *whom*?' The object is always a noun or a pronoun.

We can say that the verb *found* needs the object *boy* to complete its meaning. It is a **transitive verb**.

In the second sentence, the verb *was lying* does not have an object. It is an **intransitive verb**.

A **transitive verb** is one which needs an object to complete its meaning in a sentence.

An **intransitive verb** does not need an object to complete its meaning.

**A. Underline the verbs and state whether they are transitive or intransitive in your notebook.**

1. The dog is barking.
2. Brian locked the door.
3. The plane landed safely.
4. Rama's mother cooked a tasty meal.
5. Maryam washed her hands with soap.
6. Abhi suddenly stopped on the busy road.

comma, full stop, capital letters, exclamation mark

A **capital letter** is used to begin a sentence and in proper nouns.

A **full stop (.)** is used at the end of sentences.

A **comma (,)** is used to separate words in a sentence and between two or more words in a series.

An **exclamation mark (!)** is used at the end of sentences that show joy, sadness, or anger.

**Examples:** That feels good.

So, we came to rescue you!

Peter and Phyllis left to get help.

**B. Rewrite the sentences in your notebook using correct punctuation.**

1. help help I'm drowning
2. the eiffel tower is in France
3. my name is sarla i work in a bank
4. mahesh is going to the library today
5. if it rains we will cancel the programme
6. i want to buy a pencil sharpener and a ruler

## Study Skills

### Pronunciation

words with *al* sound

When a word has the letters *-al* in it, we can pronounce it in three ways.

- with the *al* sound, as in *palace*
- with the *el* sound, as in *tale*
- with the *all* sound, as in *salt*

**Read the words aloud. Then, write them in the correct columns on the next page.**

gale salad talent halt whale call scale almost value

| *al* as in *palace* | *al* as in *tale* | *al* as in *salt* |
|---|---|---|
| | | |

## Listening

listening for information

**Listen to a passage about three children and fill in the blanks with the correct options.**

1. The children lived in a house made of ____________.
   a. red bricks  b. yellow bricks  c. brown bricks
2. The house had ____________ in the front door.
   a. metal handles  b. coloured glass  c. a letter box
3. Peter wanted to be ____________ when he grew up.
   a. a teacher  b. a driver  c. an engineer
4. The children's mother used to ____________.
   a. write stories for them
   b. take them out for dinner
   c. work in a school
5. Their father was ____________.
   a. always angry
   b. always busy
   c. never angry and always played with them

## Speaking

giving a speech

21ST CENTURY Creativity   21ST CENTURY Communication

**Imagine that you are Jim. You have to give a speech in school on the topic 'A friend in need is a friend indeed'. You want to talk about your time in the tunnel, when Bobbie, Peter, and Phyllis rescued you.**

**You can include the following points in your speech.**

- how the children saved you, even though it was risky for them
- why people should help each other in times of trouble
- the bond of friendship that you now share with your rescuers
- how you have also sometimes helped people

## Writing

making a diary entry

21ST CENTURY Creativity

**Write a diary entry about an incident where you helped someone who was injured or was in trouble.**

**You can include these points.**

- where and how the incident happened
- how you realised that someone was in trouble
- what you did in that situation
- the dangers you faced, if any

**Useful words and phrases**

| | |
|---|---|
| thrilling | trapped |
| memory | scream |
| saved the day | rescue |
| happy to help | bandaged |

## Explore More

**Read** the story *Emil and the Detectives* by Erich Kästner. It is about the adventures of Emil who teams up with a gang of boy detectives and goes on a chase across Berlin to catch a thief.

**Watch** the film *Brave*. It is about the adventures of Merida, a princess who wants to test her skills.

folktale

6

# Robin Hood Tricks the Sheriff

### Curricular Goals

- develop a comprehensive range of vocabulary in various contexts
- develop fluency in reading and the ability to read with comprehension
- sustain effective communication skills for day-to-day interactions
- develop the ability to express themselves in writing

### Competencies

- can understand synonyms and compound words
- can use *who* or *which* to join sentences, understand the use of articles, and spell double-letter words
- can enact a conversation and write a paragraph on a subject

## Reading

**a** *Robin Hood was a folk hero who lived in Sherwood Forest in England with his band of Merry Men. Robin's biggest enemy was the dishonest and cruel Sheriff of Nottingham. Read the story to know what happened when Robin Hood met the Sheriff.*

The Sheriff of Nottingham was a very cruel man. He treated people badly. He took away their money and left them to **starve**. Sometimes, for a very small mistake, he would punish them badly. So, the poor men went to Robin Hood, who lived in Sherwood Forest. Robin gave them food and money. Some stayed with him and worked for him.

### Cross-curricular Corner

Sherwood Forest was a royal hunting forest near Nottingham in England. It was a common belief that forests were dangerous places. People travelling through forests were often robbed.

The Sheriff hated Robin for helping people. Robin often visited Nottingham. But he was always so cleverly **disguised** that the Sheriff could never catch him.

One day Robin was walking through the forest when he met a **butcher** riding to the market. On either side of his grey pony hung a basket full of meat.

'What do you have there, my man?' Robin asked.

starve: to cause someone to become weak or die by not giving them enough food

disguised: looked different to avoid recognition

butcher: a person who sells meat

'Fine mutton for the Nottingham Market. Do you want to buy some?' the butcher asked.

'Yes, I'll buy it all and your pony too. I want to go to the market and see what kind of butcher I will make,' said Robin.

The man agreed. Robin put on the butcher's blue coat and leather belt, **mounted** his pony and left.

**Cross-curricular Corner**

The stories say that Robin Hood only took money from rich people so that he could give it to the poor, who were very badly treated by the rich lords for whom they worked. So, he became famous for 'robbing from the rich and giving to the poor'.

In Nottingham, the town was very crowded. Many people had come to the market. Robin rode his pony to the corner where the butchers had their stalls.

What did Robin take from the butcher?

He laid out his meat, and began to cry out, 'Best meat, everyone. Come and buy. Cheapest in all the market. Two **pence** a **pound**.'

Everyone rushed to Robin's stall, **eager** to buy. The other butchers stood **idle**. They wondered who the man was. They worried that Robin was **ruining** their trade.

'We must find out who he is,' said the chief butcher. 'Let us invite him for dinner with us and the Sheriff today at the town hall.'

'Thank you,' said Robin, when they asked him. 'I've had a busy morning and I am very hungry.'

At the Sheriff's house, his wife welcomed them kindly.

'I hope to see you at the market again, kind sir,' she said. 'Come and see me next time you have meat to sell.'

'Thank you, lady, I will not forget your kindness,' replied Robin, with a bow.

At dinner, he sat in the place of honour on the Sheriff's right. He **chuckled** to himself thinking that he was dining with his great enemy, the Sheriff of Nottingham. If the Sheriff knew who he was, he would have put him in prison.

mounted: climbed up on a horse
pence: plural of penny, a unit of money
pound: a unit of weight
eager: want to do or have something
idle: without anything to do
ruining: spoiling
chuckled: laughed quietly

Meanwhile, the Sheriff was thinking hard. The greedy man said to himself, 'This silly fellow doesn't know the value of things. If he has any sheep and goats, I'll buy them from him for a small sum and sell them again to the butchers for a high price, and make a lot of money.'

After dinner, he took Robin **aside**.

He said, 'You seem new to this business. The butchers are all waiting to cheat you. If you have any animals to sell, come to me. I'll give you a good price.'

'I do have two or three hundred sheep and goats and a hundred **acres** of good land,' Robin replied.

How many animals did Robin say he had?

The Sheriff nearly danced with joy when he heard this.

'Now, young man, when can I see these beasts of yours?' asked the Sheriff, rubbing his hands in excitement.

'I start for home tomorrow morning,' said Robin. 'If you come with me, I will show you the animals and the land too.'

The Sheriff agreed. That night he took three hundred pounds in gold in three bags.

In the morning, the Sheriff **saddled** his horse and set out with Robin. The sun shone as they rode **merrily**. When the Sheriff saw that they were taking the road to Sherwood Forest, he began to feel nervous.

'There is a bold, bad man in these woods,' he said. 'He is called Robin Hood. He robs people. Do you think we will meet him?'

'I'm quite sure we won't,' replied Robin with a laugh.

A little deeper into the forest, Robin pointed towards a hundred head of good, fat deer. 'Look!' he said. 'What do you think of my animals?'

'These are not sheep,' said the Sheriff, in a shaky voice, 'I think I should go back to Nottingham.'

'What! And not buy any sheep? Are they not fine and fat? Come, come, Sheriff, you have brought the money for them too.'

aside: to one side
acres: a unit of measuring area
saddled: put a seat on a horse
merrily: happily

**Clutching** his bags, he said, 'This isn't money. These are only **pebbles**.'

Then Robin put his horn to his mouth and blew out three blasts. Immediately, Little John and the other Merry Men rushed out.

Who came rushing when Robin blew his horn?

'I hope you have something nice for dinner, because I've brought the Sheriff of Nottingham to dine with us,' Robin said to Little John.

'Yes,' answered Little John, 'the cooks are busy already, although we had not expected such a fine guest. I hope he'll pay us honestly.'

The Sheriff was very afraid now. He realised that he had fallen into the hands of Robin Hood. Robin always gave the men who stole from poor people a very fine dinner and made them pay a great deal of money for it.

They had a fine dinner, and the Sheriff began thinking that he would get off easily. But Robin said, 'Now, Master Sheriff, you must pay.'

### Cross-curricular Corner

The men in Robin Hood's gang had nicknames. Nicknames are humorous names given to people. For example, Little John. John was not 'little' at all, being unusually tall. He was the most famous and loyal among Robin's Merry Men. He joined Robin's group, but not before he defeated him in a fight.

'But I am a poor man and have no money,' the Sheriff cried.

'No money! What do you have in your **saddle bags** then?' asked Robin.

Little John searched the Sheriff's saddle bags, and counted out three hundred **pounds**.

'Sheriff,' said Robin angrily, 'I shall keep all this money and divide it among my men, though it is not half as much as you have stolen from them.'

The poor Sheriff shook in his shoes[1].

### Common idioms and proverbs

1. **shake in one's shoes:** to be very frightened or nervous

'I always punish people who tell lies. But your wife was kind to me yesterday,' he said. 'For her sake, I am letting you go. But if you are not good to your people, you won't escape so easily another time.' Then, Robin called for the Sheriff's pony and let the man go back.

clutching: holding
pebbles: small round stones
saddle bags: large bags hung from a saddle, laid over the back of a horse
pounds: the unit of money used in the United Kingdom

## In a Nutshell

**Who** Robin Hood, the Sheriff of Nottingham, and the butchers

**Where** Nottingham and the forest of Sherwood

**What** Robin Hood wanted to make the Sheriff pay for cheating the people.

**Why** The Sheriff was a greedy man who took the people's money.

**How** Robin Hood tricked the Sheriff and took him to the forest.

## Comprehension

ia **A. Write whether the following statements are true (T) or false (F). Write the false statements correctly in your notebook.**

1. The Sheriff was a kind man. ☐
2. Robin Hood sold the meat at a cheaper price than the other butchers. ☐
3. The butchers invited Robin Hood to have dinner with the King. ☐
4. The Sheriff planned to help Robin Hood in his business. ☐
5. The Sheriff carried pebbles in his bags. ☐

**B. Answer these questions.**

1. Where did the poor men go after being troubled by the Sherriff and why?
2. Whom did Robin Hood meet in the forest and what did they trade?
3. What did Robin Hood do with all the meat?
4. Why did the Sheriff want to buy the goats and sheep?
5. Where did the Sheriff go with Robin Hood? What happened to him there?

## Life Skills and Values

helping others

21ST CENTURY Critical Thinking

1. Why do you think Robin Hood was selling the meat so cheaply?
2. Do you think Robin Hood was right to rob the rich and give to the poor?

## Vocabulary

synonyms

Words which are similar in meaning are called **synonyms**.

**Examples:** The sun shone as they rode **merrily**.

The sun shone as they rode **happily**.

In these sentences, *merrily* and *happily* mean the same. They are synonyms.

### A. Write the synonyms of the underlined words.

present glad error thief sick cost

1. The price of this toy is too high. ____________
2. I fell ill after eating the stale food. ____________
3. Mandira made a small mistake in her paper. ____________
4. I was so happy to see my grandparents after a long time. ____________
5. The burglar broke into the house, but he found nothing valuable. ____________
6. Radha received a beautiful birthday gift from her best friend Tina. ____________

compound words

### B. Circle the word which does not form a compound noun with the words in bold.

1. **super**
   a. market b. power c. day d. man
2. **back**
   a. pack b. stage c. bone d. charge
3. **book**
   a. shelf b. way c. mark d. keeper
4. **life**
   a. water b. boat c. line d. guard
5. **fore**
   a. finger b. father c. head d. lift
6. **some**
   a. day b. paper c. one d. body

**Grammar**

using *who* or *which*

Look at these sentences.

So, the poor men went to Robin Hood, **who** lived in Sherwood Forest.

Little John searched the Sheriff's saddle bag, **which** had three hundred pounds.

We use *who* to refer to people and *which* to refer to things. In these sentences, *who* refers to Robin Hood and *which* refers to saddle bag.

We can also join sentences using *who* or *which*.

**A. Join these sentences using *who* or *which*.**

1. This is the old car. Her father sold it off.
2. This is the river. It has many colourful fish.
3. This is the vet. He gave the dog some biscuits.
4. These are the boxes. They contain Aman's toys.
5. This is the footballer. She passed the ball to Srilata.
6. This is Little John. He is Robin Hood's most loyal friend.

articles: *a*, *an*, *the*

Read these sentences.

One day Robin was walking through **the** forest when he met **a** butcher.

Robin had **an** egg, **an** apple, and **an** orange with him.

The words *a*, *an*, and *the* are articles and they are used before nouns.

We use *a* and *an* with nouns that are singular in number.

We use *a* with nouns starting with a consonant and *an* with nouns starting with a vowel.

We use *the* when we talk of a particular person or thing.

ia **B. Fill in the blanks with *a*, *an*, or *the*.**

One hot day, ______ ant went to ______ pond to drink water. But she slipped and fell into ______ pond. ______ sparrow saw ______ ant crying for help. 'I must help her', she thought. 'If I pick up ______ leaf and drop it in ______ water, ______ ant can climb on it. ______ leaf will be like ______ boat for ______ ant.' So ______ sparrow dropped ______ leaf into ______ water and ______ ant climbed on to it. ______ sparrow saved ______ ant's life.

## Study Skills

### Spelling

double-letter words

Look at these words from the story and note how they are spelt.

Sheriff mutton stall dinner pebbles

These are all double-letter words, having at least one set of letters used twice.

**Complete the double-letter words in the following sentences.**

1. I usually sleep hugging my soft pi_ _ow.
2. We have di_ _er at 8 p.m. every day.
3. I went to the ma_ _ this weekend and bought a pair of shoes.
4. I saw the little girl w_ _ping in the park.
5. The p_ _r people of the land met the king.
6. I was l_ _king for my puppy and finally found her in the garden.

## Listening

listening to a poem and gap filling

**Listen to a poem about a cunning crocodile and fill in the blanks.**

1. The crocodile is improving his ______________________.
2. He is pouring the waters of the ______________________.
3. The crocodile has ______________________ scales.
4. He seems to grin ______________________.
5. He neatly spreads his ______________________.
6. He ______________________ little fishes inside his ______________________.

### Dictation

**You will now listen to a short passage and write it down. Each sentence will be repeated twice. Listen carefully and try not to make any spelling errors.**

## Speaking

making guesses

**In the story, the butchers try to guess who Robin was. In pairs, enact this conversation.**

**Butcher 1:** Who is this man? Why is he selling the meat so cheaply? We haven't had a single customer all morning!
**Butcher 2:** He must be a fool who does not know how to do business properly. He could also be selling meat that has gone bad.

**Now, imagine you are the Sheriff of Nottingham. You are riding into Sherwood Forest not knowing that you are with Robin Hood. You begin to wonder who your companion really is and whether you are taking the correct path. Share your thoughts with the class.**

**Useful words and phrases**

- I believe...
- I think...
- Maybe...
- Perhaps...
- Could it be...?
- Is it...?

## Writing

writing a paragraph

**Robin Hood helped the poor with the money he took from the rich. What do you want to do when you grow up? Write a paragraph on the subject.**

**You can use these points in your paragraph.**

- what you want to be and the reasons for your choice
- what you will do when you become that person
- how your work would help others

## Explore More

**Read** the book *William Tell* by Leonard Everett Fisher. It tells the story of the brave William Tell, who was forced by a cruel governor to shoot an apple placed on his son's head.

**Watch** the film *The Adventures of Tintin.* It is the story of Tintin, his dog Snowy, and the various people they meet on the way.

**Listen** to the Rajasthani folk song *Ghurchari Mev Khan.* It is about a local hero who fought against the British. The song talks about his bravery.

# Project 1

**A. A collage is a picture made using magazine and newspaper clippings, photographs, pieces of coloured paper or cloth, pasted on a canvas.**

**You recently read a poem on India. Choose any one of these topics and create an interesting collage on it.**

- Different kinds of food in India
- Popular dance forms of India
- Traditional dresses from different regions of India

**Work in pairs and be creative. Also present your collage in class and share why you chose that particular topic.**

**B. The stories *The Hound in the Red Jersey* and *Robin Hood Tricks the Sheriff* are both about adventure. Look at the given treasure map. Working in pairs, read the clues and trace the path to the treasure.**

**Directions:**

1. Enter the island from the Bandit's Rock.
2. Go north, you will see a cannon. From there, turn right and walk till you reach the Marauder's Lake.
3. On your left, you will see huge mountains and on the right, will be the deep, dark lake. Keep going straight till you see two tall palm trees.
4. Go around the lake but be careful not to fall in!
5. On the other side of the lake, you will finally see the treasure chest.
6. Do not walk past it, as then you will end up in the Traitor's Swamp, where you will surely lose your way!

**Now work with your partner and design a new treasure map with directions and play the game again. You can keep changing the directions.**

UNIT IV

# Food and History

## Warm-up

**A. Read the descriptions of these common spices used in cooking. Look at the picture clues and guess the names.**

**Who Am I?**

I am a red, dried fruit, spicy in taste: *Chilli*

I have green pods with small, black, sweet seeds. I lend a nice taste and smell to desserts: ______

I am the small, black, dried berry of a plant. I am usually added to soups along with salt: ______

I am a small white bulb-like plant. I have a strong smell and I'm used in many dishes, especially Chinese: ______

I am the brown root of a plant. When had with tea, I help cure colds: ______

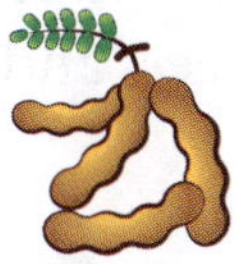

I am a sour dried fruit, which is used in chutneys and sauces: ______

**B. India is a vast country where different regions have their own food items. Think and answer these questions about the food you eat.**

1. Which region do you come from?
2. What are some of the traditional foods you eat at home?
3. Which is your favourite traditional food item?
4. Do you eat it daily or is it prepared only on special occasions? If so, what is the occasion?
5. Name any one ingredient that is used to make the dish.

poem

# 7 Eating Words

Katherine B. Hauth

### Curricular Goals

- develop a comprehensive range of vocabulary in various contexts
- develop the ability to express themselves in writing

### Competencies

- can understand antonyms and analogies
- can write a limerick

## Reading

**a** *Some creatures eat only plants and vegetables, others eat only meat, and some eat both. Do you know what each of these types of 'eaters' is called? Read this poem and find out.*

SUSTAINABLE DEVELOPMENT GOALS 15 LIFE ON LAND

When you know
that 'vore' means 'eat',
you will know
that insectivores feed
on grasshoppers, moths, and butterflies,
mosquitoes, bees, and **plain old** flies.

When you know
that herb means 'plant',
you will know
that herbivores can't
eat anything that
moves on a foot,
just foods that
**spring up** from a root.

**Cross-curricular Corner**

There are certain animals which feed on the flesh of dead animals. These animals, including vultures, hyenas, and jackals are known as scavengers. Termites, on the other hand, feed on dead plants.

When you know
that 'carni' means 'meat',
you will know
that carnivores eat
snakes and
lizards, deer and lamb,
**carrion**, birds, fish, and **clams**.

When you know
that 'omni' means 'all',
you will know
that omnivores call
Everything
they can suck or chew—
sometimes even me or you—
food.

plain old: ordinary
carrion: rotting flesh of dead animals
clams: a type of shellfish that can be eaten
spring up: grow

## In a Nutshell

**Who** Different types of animals

**What** Names of different foods eaten by animals

**How** The animals have got their names based on the foods they eat.

## About the poet

Katherine B. Hauth is an American children's author and poet. Many of her poems are inspired by her observations of animals around her. She has written poetry books like *What's for Dinner?* and *Night Life of the Yucca: The Story of a Flower and a Moth.*

## Understanding the Poem

### A. Choose the correct options.

1. The word 'vore' means
   a. eat.
   b. drink.
   c. eat and drink.
2. Insectivores are animals and plants who eat
   a. vegetables and grasshoppers.
   b. mosquitoes, butterflies, and grasshoppers.
   c. snakes and lizards.
3. Carnivores eat
   a. only vegetables.
   b. meat and vegetables.
   c. snakes and lizards, deer and lamb, birds, fish, and clams.
4. The phrase 'moves on a foot' means
   a. something which can move and walk around like animals.
   b. something which has only one foot.
   c. something which has wheels like cars.

### B. Read the lines and answer the questions.

1. *When you know/that 'vore' means 'eat',*
   *you will know...*
   a. Which type of eater is mentioned in this stanza?
   b. What are the things they eat?
   c. Mention another word in this stanza which also means 'eat'.

2. *Everything/they can suck or chew—*
   *sometimes even me or you—/food.*
   a. Which type of eaters does this stanza talk about?
   b. What kind of food do 'they' eat?
   c. Who are being referred to as 'me' and 'you' here?

## Life Skills and Values

food habits

1. Did you find the last line of the poem funny? Give reasons.
2. Are you a herbivore, carnivore, or omnivore? State with reference to the food you eat.
3. What, according to you, should be a balanced diet?

## Vocabulary

antonyms

ia **A. The antonym or opposite of the word *old* from the poem is *young*. Write the opposites using the given words.**

lose    nothing    different    give    float    confident

| | Words | Opposites |
|---|---|---|
| 1. | sink | |
| 2. | receive | |
| 3. | nervous | |
| 4. | everything | |
| 5. | same | |
| 6. | find | |

ia **B. Fill in the blanks with the opposites of the underlined words.**

1. The young boy helped the ____________ man cross the road.
2. Mira arrives early for class every day, but today she was ____________.
3. Do not take the heavy suitcase, carry the ___________ backpack instead.
4. The bottle with orange juice is quite full, but the one with the watermelon juice is almost ____________.
5. My clothes got dirty after playing football in the muddy field. After a good wash, they were ____________.

analogies

We often use an **analogy** to compare two things on the basis of a common quality they both share.

**Examples:**

animal products

animal kingdom

babies

**C. Complete the following analogies by choosing the correct options. Mention the relationship between the two.**

1. Tree is to leaf as flower is to petal. relationship: parts of a plant
   a. grass b. petal c. bark
2. Bed is to sleep as chair is to ________________.
   a. eat b. drive c. sit
3. Truck is to road as boat is to ________________.
   a. sky b. lake c. street
4. Hop is to rabbit as gallop is to ________________.
   a. cow b. cat c. horse
5. Baker is to cake as carpenter is to ________________.
   a. table b. blanket c. biscuit
6. A station is to train as an airport is to ________________.
   a. ship b. aeroplane c. bus

**Activity**

writing a limerick

A **limerick** is a funny poem in five lines.

Read the following limerick by Edward Lear.

There was an old man in a tree,
Whose whiskers were lovely to see;

But the birds of the air,
Plucked them perfectly bare,
To make themselves nests on that tree.

Did you notice how the first, second, and fifth lines rhyme? The third and fourth lines rhyme too.

Let's learn how to write a limerick.

**Limerick**

- **Line 1:** the main character and setting
- **Line 2:** the main idea of the poem, rhymes with line 1
- **Line 3:** more information about the idea, rhymes with line 4
- **Line 4:** action of the poem, rhymes with line 3
- **Line 5:** the funny 'punch line' of the poem, rhymes with lines 1 and 2

**Write a limerick on how a clever mouse fooled a cat which wanted to eat it. You can describe funny situations such as the mouse playing tricks on the cat, and the cat running around the house and tripping over household objects.**

**Useful words and phrases**

| | |
|---|---|
| mat | cat |
| hat | mouse |
| house | fell |
| tell | chase |
| maze | jumped |
| toppled | slip |
| dip | |

## Explore More

**Read** the poem *Praying Mantis* by David Harrison. It explains why a praying mantis, an insect, has to wait for its prey.

**Watch** *A Life on Our Planet*. This documentary by David Attenborough looks at nature and talks about different animals.

non-fiction

8

# Around the World with a Chilli

Nayan Chanda

### Curricular Goals

- develop a comprehensive range of vocabulary in various contexts
- develop fluency in reading and the ability to read with comprehension
- sustain effective communication skills for day-to-day interactions
- develop the ability to express themselves in writing

→

### Competencies

- can understand homophones, words related to food, and headwords in a dictionary
- can use prepositions and understand subject–verb agreement
- can speak using the correct intonation and write a recipe

## Reading

**a** *Do you enjoy chillies in your food, or do you find them too hot? Did you know that 500 years ago, no one in India knew what chillies were? Read this story about the chilli's journey to reach our shores.*

The sun had just **dipped** behind the coconut, mango and chikoo trees around Appu's house. The kitchen garden was **bathed** in a soft light. Appu's mother was making fish curry for dinner and wanted some fresh green chillies. Twelve-year-old Appu had gone to the garden to pick some when he heard a deep voice say, 'I am so glad your family likes my fruits.'

Appu turned around to see who was speaking. The voice seemed to come out of the knee-high, leafy chilli plant.

'Don't be frightened. I am **Ajar Uchu**. I am the Spirit of Chillies,' it said.

'Thank you for watering the plants every evening and taking care of them. I am thousands of miles away from home. It means a lot to me.'

Appu took a few moments to **recover** from the surprise of a plant speaking. He asked, 'Where do you come from?'

'From a place called Mexico but I am found across South America too,' Ajar Uchu answered.

Where did Ajar Uchu come from?

dipped: (here) set, sunk
bathed: (here) covered
Ajar Uchu: chilli peppers, in the Inca language
recover: (here) to get back to one's senses after a shock

Before Appu could ask where Mexico was, his mother called from the kitchen, 'Appu, please bring the chillies.'

Ajar Uchu said, 'Come back tomorrow and I'll tell you the story of our journey to India.' Still wondering, Appu nodded and ran off.

He went to his room and turned his small **globe** to see where Mexico was. He quickly found the country.

### Cross-curricular Corner

The Incas and the Aztecs made many discoveries in the fields of science and agriculture. They studied the movement of stars, and used calendars to mark festivals as well as the seasons for farming. The words 'chilli' and 'chocolate' are from the Aztec language. The Incas built Machu Pichhu, an ancient city, now a historical tourist site.

The next day, Appu carefully watered the chilli plants with their bright green and red **pods**.

'Ahh! This is so **refreshing** after a hot day!' Ajar Uchu spoke. 'Thank you, Appu. Now let me tell you my story.'

'Thousands of years ago,' Ajar Uchu said, 'the Incas ruled a part of the vast mountains and forests of South America. They grew maize, potato, tomato and many other fruits and vegetables. The Inca gods sent four brothers to help the people. I was one of the brothers. My job was to '**pepper up**' the life of the people. The chilli is actually a fruit, even though most people think of it as a vegetable. The Inca people liked chillies a lot. It made their plain food of corn flour and potatoes tasty.'

'But how did you travel from your country to India?' Appu asked. On the globe, Appu had seen that vast oceans and the **continent** of Africa lay between India and South America.

The voice said, 'The **foreigners** who came to South America and helped to take the chilli plant all over the world were actually looking for a way to reach India. Over five hundred years ago, an Italian captain named Christopher Columbus set out with three Spanish ships. They crossed the Atlantic Ocean hoping to find a shorter route to India. They did not know that the huge American continents and the Pacific Ocean stood in the way.'

'Why did they want to come to India?' Appu asked.

Where did Columbus want to go?

globe: a ball-shaped object with a map of the world on it, usually on a stand that can be turned
pods: long thin coverings filled with seeds
refreshing: (something) that makes you feel better when you are hot or tired
pepper up: to add excitement and happiness
continent: one of the large land masses of the earth such as Europe, Asia, or Africa
foreigners: people from another country

Ajar Uchu replied, 'They wanted pepper, which grew only in India. The Europeans loved adding it to their food. When he landed, Columbus was sure that he had reached India. So he called the Aztec, Inca and other local people he met 'Indians'.'

### Literary term

1. This is a **simile**, where chillies are being compared to Indian pepper.

'Columbus was very disappointed that the people in the new lands had no black pepper to sell. But they showed him various types of chilli. He tasted them and found that the chillies were as hot and spicy as Indian pepper[1]. He took them back to Spain,' said Ajar Uchu.

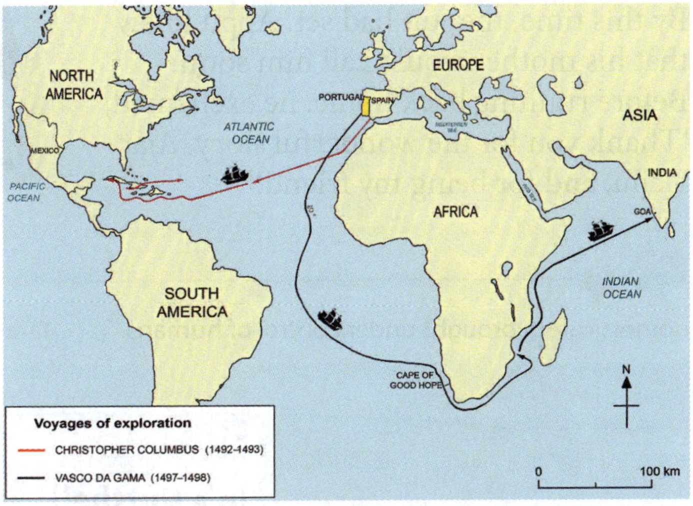


'Columbus came to look for *kali mirch* and took home *hari mirch* and *lal mirch* instead!' Appu laughed.

'It was the explorer Vasco da Gama who reached India, six years later,' Ajar Uchu continued. 'He led four Portuguese ships around the tip of Africa and reached a place called Calicut.'

'Vasco da Gama wanted to take away some pepper plants to his country. But the plants could not be grown in the **climate** of Europe. So, the Portuguese decided to settle in India and **trade** in spices and other goods. They captured Goa and turned it into a great **trading post**. They sent huge amounts of pepper to Europe.'

### Cross-curricular Corner

The Bhut jolokia, also known as ghost pepper, was named the world's hottest chili pepper by the Guinness World Records in 2007. It is grown in the states of Arunachal Pradesh, Assam, Nagaland, and Manipur.

'Goa! It was the world's **gateway** to India. While large sailing ships left Goa loaded with pepper and other spices, the Portuguese brought in new items from South America. Among them was the chilli. When chilli seeds arrived in Goa, they immediately became popular. It added a lot of flavour to the food.

Why do Bengalis call chillies 'lanka'?

The people passed the hot chilli peppers and it spread to all over western India. Soon, different varieties of chillies – long, round, fat and of different colours – reached India and Sri Lanka. From Sri Lanka, the chilli reached Bengal. Maybe that's why Bengalis call chilli *lanka*,' said Ajar Uchu.

climate: the pattern of weather conditions
trade: to buy and sell things
trading post: a small place or a store where trading is done
gateway: a place leading to a larger place

'So that is how one of the earliest wild plants to be **domesticated** by humans in **faraway** South America nearly 9,000 years ago became an important food item that spread to many parts of the world. Do you see how the world is connected by the food we eat?' said Ajar Uchu.

By this time, the sun had set. Appu knew that his mother would call him soon. Before running back home, he exclaimed, 'Thank you for the wonderful story, Ajar Uchu, and for being my friend!'

domesticated: brought under control of humans    faraway: a long way away

### In a Nutshell

**Who** Appu, a young boy and Ajar Uchu, a chilli

**When** In the evening

**What** Ajar Uchu told Appu the story about its journey to India.

**How** Ajar Uchu and other chillies travelled from Mexico to other parts of the world with Portuguese sailors.

## Comprehension

### A. Fill in the blanks with words from the story.

1. Ajar Uchu had come from a place called ______________, but was also found across ______________.
2. The chilli is actually a ______________, even though most people think of it as a vegetable.
3. Columbus called the ______________ and the ______________ 'Indians'.
4. Vasco da Gama wanted to take away some ______________ plants to his country.
5. ______________ was the world's gateway to India.

**B. Answer these questions.**

1. Who was Ajar Uchu?
2. Where did the Incas live and what did they grow?
3. What lay between South America and India?
4. Why did foreigners go to South America?
5. Describe Vasco da Gama's journey to India.
6. Why did the Portuguese decide to settle in India?

## Life Skills and Values

community bonding

21ST CENTURY Critical Thinking

1. When the Portuguese settled in India, what effect did it have on Indian food?
2. Ajar Uchu felt that we are all connected by the food that we eat. Do you agree with the statement? Give examples from the story to support your answer.

## Vocabulary

homophones

The words **chilli** and **chilly** have the same pronunciation but their meanings and spellings are different. **Chilli** refers to a type of pepper, while **chilly** refers to a condition when we feel extremely cold. The two words are **homophones**.

ia **A. Fill in the blanks with the correct homophones.**

1. Please don't ______________ (waist/waste) water.
2. I ______________ (made/maid) a bird using craft paper.
3. Early in the morning, there was ______________ (dew/due) on the grass.
4. Anita was preparing the ______________ (doe/dough) for baking the cookies.
5. My parents bought me a new ______________ (pair/pear) of shoes for school.
6. My brothers were quarrelling over the last ______________ (peace/piece) of apple pie.

words related to food

There are various food-related words in the story.

**Examples:** It made their **plain** food of corn flour and potatoes **tasty**.
It added a lot of **flavour** to the food.

### ia B. Fill in the blanks with the correct options.

1. I like to have ___toasted___ (salted/toasted) bread for breakfast.
2. Freshly-baked bread is ______________ (crunchy/fluffy).
3. The potato fries were ______________ (dripping/grilling) with oil.
4. You should ______________ (peel/chop) the orange before you eat it.
5. My mother makes buttermilk with homemade ______________ (curd/cheese).
6. Mani forgot the mangoes in the shopping bag. A week later, he found that they had got ______________ (spoilt/burnt).

## Grammar

prepositions

Read these sentences.

The sun had just dipped **behind** the coconut trees **around** Appu's house.

The words *behind* and *around*, which show where someone or something is, are known as prepositions.

**Prepositions** are words which show the connection between a noun or pronoun and other words in a sentence. They can tell us about time, place, and movement.

Some other common prepositions are *at, in, above, below, up, down, before,* and *after.*

### ia A. Fill in the blanks with the correct prepositions.

1. Meeta walked ______________ (beside/across) her father.
2. The cat jumped ______________ (into/over) the baby's toys.
3. Arun put all the wastepaper ______________ (under/in) the bin.
4. Watch out! There's a monkey ______________ (behind/along) you.
5. The thief swam ______________ (across/over) the river and ran away.
6. I was feeling so cold that I quickly slipped ______________ (under/above) the blanket.

You know what the subject in a sentence is. It can be singular or plural.

In a sentence, the verb must always agree with the subject in number and person. If the subject is singular, the verb must also be singular. If the subject is plural, then the verb must also be plural. This is known as the **agreement of the subject and the verb**.

**Examples:** Your family **likes** my fruits. (singular subject: *family*; singular verb: *likes*)

The foreigners **were** actually **looking** for a way to reach India.

(plural subject: *foreigners*; plural verb: *were looking*)

**B. Fill in the blanks with the correct options.**

1. The librarian ______________ (is/are) reading a book.
2. She ______________ (is/are) working on the computer.
3. Sita and Sana ______________ (is/are) in the same class.
4. Rana and Meeta ______________ (is/are) playing football.
5. My friends always ______________ (shares/share) their toys with me.
6. Every morning, my father and I ______________ (goes/go) for a walk.

## Study Skills

### Dictionary Skills

headwords

Look at the dictionary entry for the word *charge*.

headword ← **charge** charges, charging, charged → derived forms

meaning: VERB **1** if someone **charges** you money, they ask you to pay for something.
VERB **2** if something or someone **charges** towards you, they rush forward.

other usage: **in charge** PHRASE if you are **in charge** of something, you are the person looking after it.

A **headword** is a word in a dictionary whose meaning is given. It is usually given in bold.

**Write the headwords and meanings for these travel-related words, using a dictionary. One has been done for you.**

| Word | Headword | Meaning |
|---|---|---|
| 1. toured | *tour* | *went on a journey or a trip* |
| 2. sightseeing | | |
| 3. enjoyable | | |
| 4. camping | | |
| 5. departure | | |
| 6. excitedly | | |

## Listening

listening to a passage and matching facts

**Listen to a passage about the origin of sugar and then match the information given in the columns correctly.**

| Column A | Column B |
|---|---|
| 1. Darius, the Persian emperor | a. to use in trade. |
| 2. One of the earliest plants that Indians grew | b. attacked India in 510 B.C. |
| 3. Dried sugar bits were easy to carry around | c. he sent a few people to India to learn how to make sugar. |
| 4. The Buddhist monks took sugar | d. was sugarcane. |
| 5. The Chinese emperor was so impressed that | e. to China from India. |

## Speaking

using correct intonation

When we ask questions, our voice falls from a higher to a lower level.

**A. Working in pairs, practise saying these questions aloud. Say the question words with more stress than the other words.**

1. *What* is your name? 2. *Where* do you stay? 3. *When* did you wake up today?

When we answer questions, our voice rises from a lower to a higher level.

**B. Now, take turns to answer the questions you just asked. Say the last word in the sentence with more stress than the rest.**

1. My name is __________.
2. I stay in __________.
3. I woke up at __________ today.

C. **With your partner, write three questions of your own and take turns to ask and answer them.**

**You can ask questions about the following.**

- pets
- games
- favourite books

## Writing

writing a recipe

21ST CENTURY Creativity

**Work in pairs and write down the recipe for a fruit salad. Include the following points in your recipe.**

- a list of the items you need
- the process for making the salad
- the time you need

**Useful words and phrases**

| **For the list of ingredients:** | **For the method of preparation:** |
| --- | --- |
| a piece of, a slice of, a cup of, a teaspoon of, a dash of, some/few | cut, peel, add, mix, pour, toss bowl, plate, spoons |

## Explore More

**Read** the European folktale *The Stone Soup*. It describes how a young man tricks an old woman into believing that a delicious soup can be made with a stone.

**Listen** to *Eat Your Rainbow*. It is a fun song about vegetables and fruits, and the nutrients they contain.

# UNIT V In the Forest

**Warm-up**

SUSTAINABLE DEVELOPMENT GOALS 15 LIFE ON LAND

21ST CENTURY Critical Thinking

**A. Read the given facts and write the names of the animals.**

It is found in parts of north and central India. The males have long horns called antlers. When it senses danger, it raises its tail to warn others in the group.

2. D ____________

It has shaggy black hair. It is known to eat honey and fruits. It has a very good sense of smell.

3. B ____________

1. E ____________

This huge animal has a long trunk and big ears. It is illegally hunted for its tusks which were once used for making furniture and showpieces.

It is the national animal of India. It has an orange coat with black stripes. It is a good swimmer.

4. R ____ B ____ T ____

This huge beast is hunted for its horn. It is a herbivore and is found in the northern parts of Uttar Pradesh, Bihar, West Bengal, and in Assam.

6. R ____________

In India, it is found in Gujarat. It is the king of the jungle. The males have a large mane.

5. L ____________

**B. Rabbits eat grass, and tigers eat rabbits. This connection between living creatures, based on food, is called a food chain. Complete the following food chains, choosing from the given options. The (⟶) stands for *eaten by*.**

fox penguin grasshopper shark chicken man fish

1. plant ⟶ worm ⟶ ______ ⟶ ______
2. grass ⟶ ______ ⟶ bird ⟶ ______
3. water plants ⟶ ______ ⟶ ______ ⟶ ______

adventure story

# 9 Trapped by a Tiger

Ruskin Bond

## Curricular Goals

- develop a comprehensive range of vocabulary in various contexts
- develop fluency in reading and the ability to read with comprehension
- sustain effective communication skills for day-to-day interactions
- develop the ability to express themselves in writing

## Competencies

- can understand animal idioms and different tenses of verbs
- can say words with long and short *o* sounds, and *oa* and *ow* sounds
- can narrate and write a short story

## Reading

**a** *Have you ever visited a forest? What would you do if you came face to face with a wild animal? Read this story of a young boy who is visited by a tiger in his house.*

I grew up at a time when hunting wild animals was a **pastime**. It was supposed to prove how strong you were. But from the beginning, I hated the so-called 'sport of kings'.

When I was twelve, one of my uncles, along with his friends, took me on a weekend's ***shikar*** in the forests near Dehra, a small north Indian town.

### Cross-curricular Corner

In 1972, a law was made to protect animal and plant species. Under the Wildlife Protection Act, nobody could kill animals for pleasure anymore and hunting was banned.

These forests were full of tigers, wild elephants and various species of deer. The hunters decided to stay at a small forest **rest house** in the **heart** of the jungle. From there they set out early every morning to the forest, returning late in the afternoon.

I had brought a couple of books along. They did not ever ask me to join them and I was grateful for that. They left me with sandwiches and a thermos of tea. I was also told by my uncle to not leave the rest house. In case I needed anything, he told me to go to the **caretaker** who lived in a hut at the other end of the **clearing**.

pastime: hobby
*shikar*: hunting, in Hindi
rest house: a house that you can pay to stay in like a hotel room
heart: (here) middle
caretaker: a person who takes care of buildings or farm lands
clearing: an open space in a forest

'It's perfectly safe here,' said Uncle Jim. 'Just don't go into the forest on your own.'

I was quite happy to see the hunting party **march off** into the jungle. I settled into an armchair on the veranda, read a little, ate a sandwich and then fell asleep in the hot April sunshine.

What did the boy see when he woke up?

I must have slept for ten or fifteen minutes. I woke up with a strong animal smell in the air. I looked up. A **monstrous** tiger was standing some thirty to forty metres away and looking directly at me.

**Common idioms and proverbs**

**the tiger cannot change its stripes:** one cannot change one's true nature, however much one pretends

I could hear my heart thumping very loudly. The tiger was silent and was watching me. I got out of my chair very quietly, **dashed** into the living room, shut the front door and locked it. I then went to the nearest window and looked out.

The tiger had walked up a few steps. Raising its head, it **sniffed** at the air. Where was that forest guard? Where were Uncle Jim and his great hunters? Just then, I realized that I was staring out of an open window. I shut it quickly. The tiger had turned away from the veranda and was circling the house.

Although confused and frightened, I remembered that the back door of the bathroom was open. I rushed and tumbled into one of the bedrooms and shut the door with a bang. The noise **startled** the tiger, and he let out an angry roar.

I raced to the second bedroom and into the bathroom and locked the door. I was trembling as I walked to the bedroom and sat down on the bed. When I looked around, I noticed that the bedroom's large window without bars was half open!

I went up to it and peeped over the **sill**. The tiger was in the backyard, much closer to the house. I could smell it. Softly, I closed the window and locked it. I returned to the living room and thought I was safe. Just then there was a heavy thump[1] on the front door, followed by an angry **snarl**. I could hear the beast's claws banging

**Literary term**

1. This is an example of **onomatopoeia**. When something solid is hit, the deep sound is just like the word 'thump'.

march off: to walk away
monstrous: large and frightening
dashed: ran with force
sniffed: smelled
startled: surprised
sill: a flat piece, usually of wood, forming the base of a window frame
snarl: growl

against the wooden door. I leapt to the closed window and put my face to the glass, and was just able to see a portion of the terrible creature.

I was shaking all over. High up on the living room wall was a small **skylight**, opening on to the roof. If I could reach it, I would climb on to the roof and be safe.

I quickly pulled the dining table across the room, placed a smaller table on top of it and then put a **cane** chair. I climbed up on the **wobbling** chair.

Meanwhile, the tiger was making a lot of noise, pushing against the door and tearing at the wood with its powerful claws.

I quickly climbed through the skylight and was out on the flat roof of the **bungalow** when I heard a big crash as the door broke down. The tiger was in the living room! I looked down through the open skylight as it circled the small room, **lashing** its tail and knocking over tables and chairs.

How did the boy reach the skylight?

In its anger, it turned its attention to my thermos flask, and bit right through it! And then it **charged out** of the living room. I watched it from the roof as it let out a big roar.

At the same time I heard a gun being fired, and the forest guard came out from his **hutment**. The tiger turned away from the bungalow and ran away into the jungle.

'Are you all right, *baba*?' asked the guard, as he helped me down from the roof.

'I think so,' I said.

An hour or two later the hunters returned, a tired **bunch**. They hadn't shot anything except for a few **pheasants**. They looked rather foolish when they heard about the tiger's visit and saw the damage it had done.

I didn't say much, because I was still in shock. Uncle Jim was glad to find me alive. It was some time before I could mention this incident to anyone as it took me a long time to **get over** it!

skylight: a small window in a roof, usually with a latch
cane: a type of plant used to make furniture
wobbling: shaking from side to side because of poor balance
bungalow: a house built all on one level
lashing: hitting with great force
charged out: moved out in a rush
hutment: a hut or group of huts, in an army camp
bunch: (here) a group
pheasants: large birds with round bodies and long tails
get over: to recover from

## In a Nutshell

| | |
|---|---|
| **Who** | The narrator, a tiger, Uncle Jim, and a forest officer |
| **When** | When the narrator was twelve years old |
| **Where** | A forest near Dehra |
| **What** | The tiger tried to attack the narrator but he escaped. |
| **How** | By climbing on the roof |

### About the author

Ruskin Bond (b. 1934) is an Indian author of British origin. He is best-known for his short stories set in Himalayan towns. Some of his most-loved stories are *Harold the Hornbill* and *Tiger in the Tunnel*.

## Comprehension

ia **A. Write whether the following statements are true (T) or false (F). Write the false statements correctly in your notebook.**

1. The hunters stayed in a forest rest house. ☐
2. The boy was sad to see the hunting party leave without him. ☐
3. The boy saw a baby tiger standing and staring at him. ☐
4. The boy was out on the flat roof of the bungalow when the tiger came in. ☐
5. The forest guard came inside the bungalow to save the boy. ☐
6. The hunters had shot a few pheasants. ☐

**B. Answer the questions and revisit the sequence of the story.**

1. What did the boy do when the hunters left?
2. What did the boy do when he saw the tiger?
3. What was the tiger doing at the beginning?
4. Why did the boy run to the bedrooms?
5. How did the boy feel once he was able to close the doors?
6. How did the tiger try to enter the house?
7. What did the boy do to reach the skylight?
8. Once the boy reached the roof, what did the tiger do?

## Life Skills and Values

responsible behaviour towards nature and others

1. Earlier, hunting was thought to be a sport which showed one's strength and bravery. Now, it is largely illegal in India. Do you think that hunting animals proves how strong or brave someone is? Why/Why not?
2. Do you think Uncle Jim was a responsible person, leaving his nephew all alone in the middle of a forest? Give reasons for your answer.

## Vocabulary

contextual usage

**A. Fill in the blanks with these words from the story. You may have to make some changes.**

startle tremble sniff tumble pastime crash

1. My grandfather's favourite ________ is painting.
2. A sudden shadow across the window ________ me at night.
3. The cat pulled the tablecloth and all the glasses ________ to the floor.
4. Neeraj missed a step while climbing down the stairs and ________ over.
5. Pramit was ________ as he tried to find his way out of the haunted house.
6. When I take my dog out on walks, he ________ the ground in search of bones.

animal idioms

Look at this idiom related to tigers.

He claimed that his enemies were **paper tigers** and not to be feared.
(paper tiger: a person or thing that seems powerful but is not so in reality)

**B. Match these animal idioms to their meanings.**

| Idioms | Meanings |
|---|---|
| 1. at a snail's pace | a. notice or see everything |
| 2. busy as a bee | b. be patient |
| 3. have eyes like a hawk | c. be nervous |
| 4. hold your horses | d. face a difficult situation with courage |
| 5. have butterflies in your stomach | e. extremely busy |
| 6. take the bull by the horns | f. someone who seems friendly but is actually dangerous |
| 7. wolf in sheep's clothing | g. very slowly |

**C. Complete the sentences using the idioms you have just learnt. You may have to make some changes.**

1. The king does not trust his minister as he is a ______________________.
2. The cars are moving ______________________ because of the heavy rains.
3. My mother has been working all day. She is ______________________.
4. Although Neha was nervous, she decided to ______________________ and tell the teacher the truth.
5. Ratna is giving a speech for the first time, and she ______________________.
6. ______________________! There is no need to rush.
7. The teacher who gave us the test today ______________________. Nothing went unnoticed by her.

## Grammar

simple past tense

Read the sentence.

I **returned** to the living room and **thought** I **was** safe.

The verbs *returned*, *thought*, and *was* are in the simple past tense.

The **simple past tense** describes an action that has been completed in the past.

**A. Fill in the blanks with the simple past tense of the given verbs.**

1. Rama __________ (buy) five packets of chips yesterday.
2. We __________ (go) to the amusement park last weekend.
3. The vase __________ (fall) and __________ (break) into pieces.
4. My mother __________ (bake) a cake for my birthday yesterday.
5. Priyam __________ (be) very scared after watching a horror film.
6. Vibhu __________ (write) a letter to his cousin and __________ (mail) it.

past continuous tense

Read these sentences.

The tiger **was watching** me. I **was staring** out of an open window.

The verbs *was watching* and *was staring* are in the past continuous tense.

The **past continuous tense** tells us about an action that continued in the past for some time.

**B. Fill in the blanks with the past continuous tense of the given verbs.**

1. Rachna ________________ (paint) all day yesterday.
2. The peacock ________________ (dance) happily in the rain.
3. We ________________ (walk) home when it started drizzling.
4. Last Sunday, while I ________________ (wait) for my bus, I met my cousin.
5. Sanket ________________ (have) dinner when his mother returned from work.
6. Sheena ________________ (play) the piano when she heard a knock on the door.

## Study Skills

### Pronunciation

long and short *o* sounds

The letter *o* has a long sound, as in *go, close*, and a short sound, as in *sock, mop*.

**A. Read the words aloud. Write the words with the long *o* sound under *rose* and those with the short *o* sound under *box*.**

| lower | octopus | stroller | olive | decode |
|---|---|---|---|---|
| comment | ocean | monster | snowman | dolphin |

| long *o* as in *rose* | short *o* as in *box* |
|---|---|
| | |

*oa* and *ow* sounds

The letter *o* combines with the letter *a* to form the sound *oa*, as in *goal, coat*, and combines with the letter *w* to form the sound *ow*, as in *snow, glow*.

**B. Look at the pictures. Write the names of each object using *oa* or *ow*.**

1. 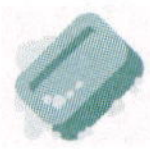 ______________________
2.  ______________________
3.  ______________________
4.  ______________________
5.  ______________________
6. 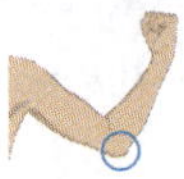 ______________________
7.  ______________________
8.  ______________________

## Listening

listening and marking directions on a map

**Listen to the directions and mark them correctly in this map.**

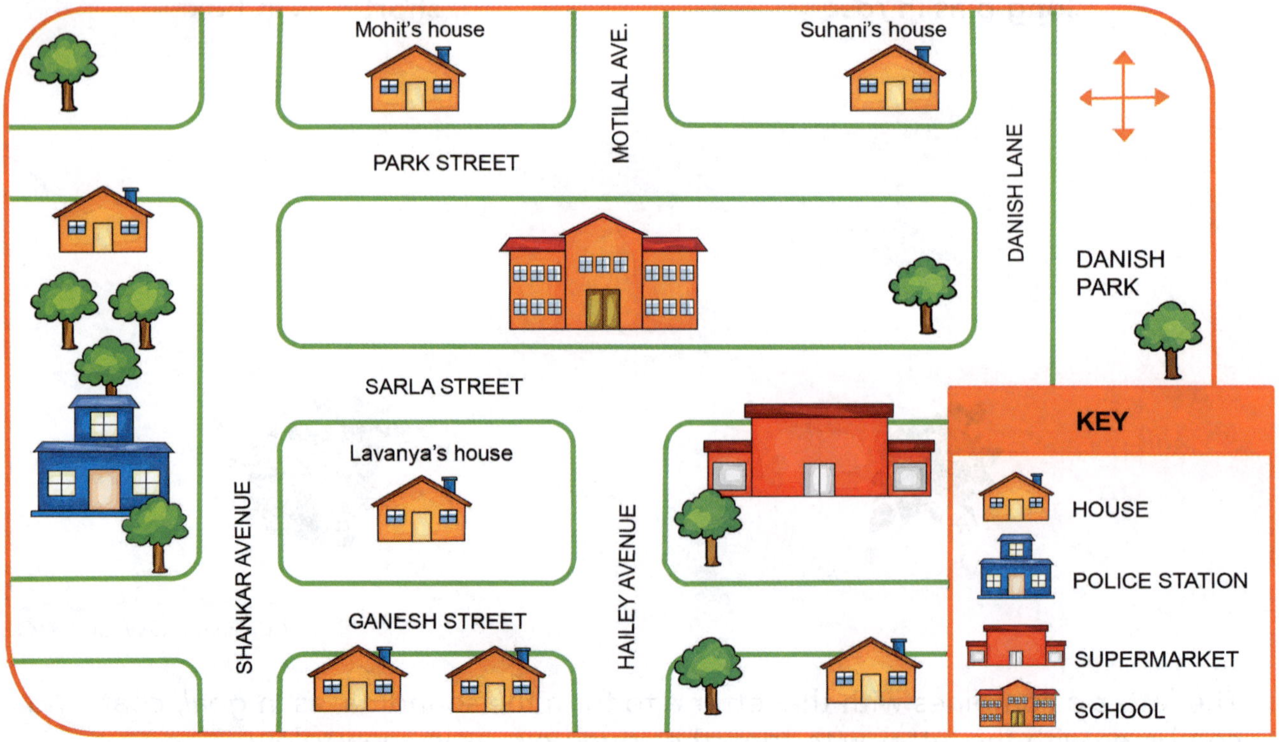

## Speaking

narrating a short story based on a proverb

A **proverb** is a well-known phrase or sentence that gives advice or says something that is generally true.

In the story, the boy faces a tiger and escapes unhurt. We can apply the proverb *fortune favours the brave* to his situation. While the boy showed courage in the face of danger, luck was also on his side, as he made it to the roof in the nick of time.

**Using any one of the given situations, narrate a story which illustrates the proverb *fortune favours the brave*.**

1. A drowning child – nobody around – man rushes to save him – being brave and risking his own life – people hear cries for help – save them
2. An explorer – curious about the world – wants to find new sea routes – sets off on a voyage – storm at sea – gives up hope – in the morning, spots land – new people and opportunities for trade

## Writing

writing a short story

Before writing a short story, ask these questions.

- What is the story about?
- What is the name/title of the story?
- Where does the story take place?
- When does it take place?
- Who are the people in the story? What are their names?
- How do the people look? What do they wear?
- Is there a problem? What happens to the people? How do they overcome the problem?
- Does the story have a happy ending?

If there is an outline for a story, it becomes easier to write it. You can keep these points in mind when developing the outline.

- Write complete sentences in the outline.
- Use the past tense in the sentences.

- Add dialogues for conversation.
- Add descriptions for the places and people.

**Now, write a short story using the given clues. Remember to use descriptive words and dialogues to make the story interesting.**

**You can use these hints:**

Rani goes to the zoo with her family – hears that a monkey has escaped – finds the monkey in a far corner – she remembers a story about a monkey and a cap seller – she tricks the monkey – it goes back into its cage – everyone praises Rani

## Explore More

**Read** the book *The Jungle Book*. It is a collection of stories by Rudyard Kipling that describes the adventures of a boy who is brought up by wolves in a forest.

**Watch** the film *Life of Pi*. It is about the adventures of a young boy who travels from Pondicherry to Canada on a boat with a tiger called Richard Parker.

poem 10

# Rainforest

Valerie Bloom

### Curricular Goals

- develop a comprehensive range of vocabulary in various contexts
- develop the ability to express themselves in writing

### Competencies

- can understand collective nouns and word associations
- can create an information chart

## Reading

**a** *A wide variety of plants and animals are found in a rainforest. Read the poem to learn how humans are destroying the beauty of a rainforest.*

There is a place where it rains a lot,
Where trees grow straight and tall,
This is the place where the sun shines hot,
And the **howler monkeys** call.

There is a place where fallen leaves
And tree trunks cover the ground,
This is the place where the wet soil **heaves**
As beetles **scamper** around.

There is a place where banana trees,
Giant figs and palm trees grow,
This is the place where you can **feast** on lychees,
Avocados and juicy mango.

howler monkeys: monkeys found in the Amazon rainforest and named after their loud, howling cry
heaves: moves up and down with regular movement
scamper: to move quickly with small, light steps
feast: to eat a large amount of food

This is the place where the **orchid blooms**,
Home of **toucan** and **macaw**,
The **capped heron** with milk-white **plumes**,
The green snake and **black mamba**.

There is a place where folks make their home,
Where they hunt and fish and farm,
This is the place from which medicines come,
Which **heal** diseases like a **charm**.

This is the place that is trying
To **survive** the tractor's roar,
This is the place that is dying,
A place that will soon be no more.

orchid: a plant with brightly coloured, unusually shaped flowers
blooms: (here) grows
toucan: a South American bird with a large brightly-coloured beak
macaw: a large American parrot having a long tail and extremely bright-coloured feathers
capped heron: a water bird found in the South American rainforest with a blue face and beak, white body and feathers, and a black head
plumes: large, soft bird's feathers
black mamba: an extremely poisonous snake
heal: (here) make healthy or normal again
charm: (here) a magical spell
survive: continue to live after being close to death

### In a Nutshell

**What** A rainforest getting destroyed by people

**How** People hunt, fish, farm, make medicines, and cut down trees.

### About the poet

Valerie Bloom (b. 1956) is a poet and novelist, born in Jamaica and settled in the UK. She writes poems for all ages. Her most notable novels are *Surprising Joy* and *The Tribe*.

## Understanding the Poem

**A. Complete the sentences with words or phrases from the poem.**

1. The fallen ______________ and ______________ cover the ground.
2. The ______________ has milk-white plumes.
3. People get medicines from the rainforest to heal ______________.
4. The ______________ is trying to survive the tractor's roar.
5. Banana trees, ______________, and ______________ grow in the rainforest.

**B. Read the lines and answer the questions.**

1. *This is the place where the wet soil heaves*
   *As beetles scamper around.*
   a. Which place is the poet referring to?
   b. Why do the beetles scamper around?
   c. What does the poet mean by 'wet soil heaves'?
2. *This is the place that is dying,*
   *A place that will soon be no more.*
   a. Which is the place?
   b. Why is the place 'dying'?
   c. What does the poet mean by 'no more'?

## Life Skills and Values

protecting rainforests and wildlife

1. Does the poem have a happy ending? Explain your answer with examples from the poem.
2. How are humans destroying the rainforest? How can we change that?

## Vocabulary

collective nouns

A **collective noun** is a collection of persons, animals, or things.

**Example:** A forest of trees is cut down.

**A. Complete the phrases using suitable collective nouns from the box. Then, use any five of them in sentences of your own.**

| tower | team | pack | gang | bunch |
|---|---|---|---|---|
| stack | litter | band | crew | school |

1. a __________ of wolves
2. a __________ of puppies
3. a __________ of grapes
4. a __________ of sailors
5. a __________ of athletes
6. a __________ of musicians
7. a __________ of giraffes
8. a __________ of fish
9. a __________ of robbers
10. a __________ of books

word associations

When a particular word is said, there are certain related words which immediately come to one's mind. This is known as **word association**.

**Example:** If we take the word forest, the associated words can be trees, grass, green, leaves, beetles, monkeys, and snakes.

**B. Fill in the blanks with suitable words associated with the words in bold.**

1. A glass of <u>cool</u> **lemonade** makes one feel refreshed.
2. The __________ in this **pen** has completely dried up.
3. The days are so __________ during the **summer** months.
4. The **medicine** you gave me for my cough is so __________.
5. The __________ of this **book** is known to be a funny person.
6. The __________ blew the whistle and the **football** match ended.

## Activity

creating an information chart

Creativity

Collaboration

**In this poem, you read about a rainforest, the animals that live there, the plants that grow there, and what humans get from the forest. Now, work in groups of four to create an information chart to be displayed in class. This chart should be about any wild animal of your choice.**

This chart should have a picture and details of the wild animal, as shown.

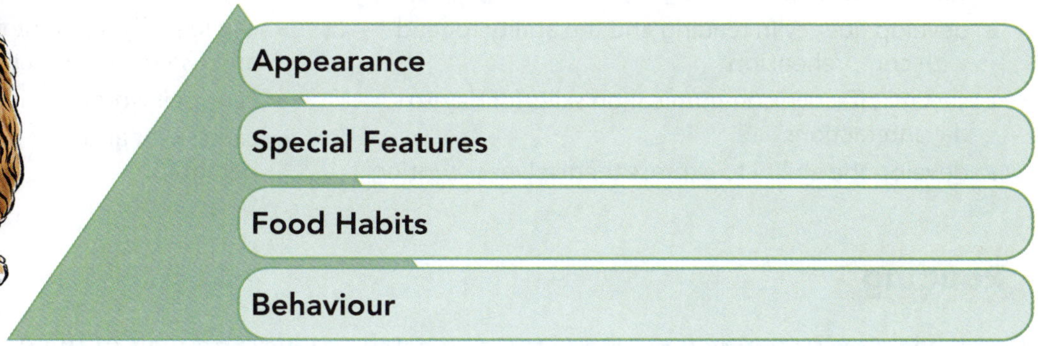


## Explore More

**Read** the story *Tree of Life*. It is about forests from Venezuela where lost children are helped by the trees in the forest.

**Listen** to the song *The Trees* by Rush. It talks about different types of trees in the forest.

play

# 11 Peter and the Wolf

Diane Redmond

## Curricular Goals

- develop a comprehensive range of vocabulary in various contexts
- develop fluency in reading and the ability to read with comprehension
- sustain effective communication skills for day-to-day interactions
- develop the ability to express themselves in writing

## Competencies

- can understand suffixes and character adjectives
- can identify different types of adverbs and use the conjunctions *because* and *so*
- can spell words ending in *-er* and *-ar*
- can ask for and give advice and write a paragraph

## Reading

**a** *Peter was a brave young boy who wanted to catch the big, bad wolf in the meadows. His grandfather was cross when he went to the meadows, but Peter had a plan. Read the play to know if he succeeded in catching the wolf.*

SUSTAINABLE DEVELOPMENT GOALS 15 LIFE ON LAND

### Characters

- Narrator
- Peter
- Grandfather
- Hunter
- Bird
- Duck
- Cat
- Wolf

**Scene 1: Peter's Cottage**

**Narrator:** Peter lived with his grandfather in a small cottage in the middle of a forest. In front of the cottage lay a big, green meadow.

**Grandfather:** Don't play in the meadow, Peter. There's a wolf out there waiting to **gobble** you up.

**Peter:** [*crossly*] Humph! Who's afraid of the big, bad wolf? NOT ME! I'm going into the meadow – it's my favourite place to play.

Name Peter's favourite place to play.

**Scene 2: The Meadows**

**Narrator:** Peter ran into the meadow and met his friend, Bird.

**Bird: Tweet**! Hello, Peter. Have you come to play with me?

**Cross-curricular Corner**

Meadows are usually man-made habitats. There are many varieties of plants and animals that live in meadows.

gobble: to eat quickly and greedily

tweet: a short, high-picthed sound made by a bird

**Peter:** [*bravely*] No. I'm going into the wood to catch the big, bad wolf.

[*A duck comes* **waddling** *into the meadow.*]

**Duck:** Quack! Quack! Don't go into the wood, Peter. Come and have a swim with me.

**Narrator:** Duck waddled into the water and started to splash about. Bird thought she looked very funny and laughed at her.

**Bird:** TWEET! What kind of bird are you if you can't fly?

**Duck:** Quack! Quack! What kind of bird are you if you can't swim?

**Bird:** TWEET! TWEET!

**Duck:** QUACK! QUACK!

**Narrator:** Bird and Duck were **arguing** so much, they didn't see Cat come **creeping up**. Cat **pounced** at Bird ...

**Narrator:** ... but Bird flew up into the branches of a tall tree.

**Bird:** Nah, nah, nah-nah, nah! You can't catch me.

**Cat:** [*crossly*] I don't care. I'll eat Duck instead.

**Peter:** Don't be silly. Duck's in the middle of the pond and you can't swim.

**Cat:** Miaow! Well, I'll climb the tree and get Bird.

[*Cat stares at Bird at the top of the tree.*]

**Peter:** [*laughing*] By the time you get up there, Bird will have flown away.

**Cat:** Miaow! I'll get you later.

**Narrator:** Suddenly Grandfather ran into the meadow, waving his arms. He looked very **cross**.

**Grandfather:** [*angrily*] Peter! I told you not to play in the meadow. It's a dangerous place!

waddling: walking with short, quick steps

arguing: speaking angrily with someone while disagreeing

creeping up (on): moving closer to someone without being seen by them

pounced: (here) jumped on another animal to hold or kill it

cross: angry

**Peter:** [*grumpily*] But Grandfather, I'm looking for the big, bad wolf.

**Grandfather:** That's enough! Go straight to your room and stay there!

**Scene 3: The Edge of the Forest**

**Narrator:**As soon as Peter and Grandfather had gone, a big, grey wolf came creeping out of the forest.

**Wolf:** Ha ha ha! Peter's gone. Now I can catch my dinner! [*The wolf creeps up on Cat.*]

**Narrator:** When Cat saw the wolf she jumped up into the tree.

**Cat:** MIAOW! MIAOOOOW!

**Narrator:** The wolf ran over to the pond. Duck saw the wolf, so she waddled out of the pond and tried to run away through the forest.

**Duck:** QUACK! QUACK!

**Wolf:** Yummy! Duck dinner for me!

Why did Duck try to run away from the wolf?

[*Duck runs away from the wolf, but he catches up with her.*]

**Duck:** [*panting for breath*] Ah... ah... ah! I can't run any faster.

**Narrator:** The **wicked** wolf **snapped** hold of Duck's tail ... and with one big **gulp**, he swallowed her up.

**Wolf:** Gulp! **Slurp**! **Slobber**!

**Narrator:** High up in the tree, Cat and Bird looked down at the wolf. The wolf looked up at them.

**Wolf:** [*licking his lips*] Yoo-hoo! I'm coming to get you, too.

**Common idioms and proverbs**

1. **to teach someone a lesson:** to punish someone so that they do not do it again

**Narrator:** But Peter had seen everything. He climbed out of his bedroom window and ran back to the forest, carrying a strong rope.

**Peter:** [*whispering to himself*] I'm going to teach that wicked wolf a lesson[1].

[*Peter scrambles up the tree where Bird and Cat are sitting.*]

**Peter:** [*in a low voice*] Bird, go and fly around the wolf's head.

**Bird:** TWEEET! No, he'll eat me.

wicked: not good, evil
snapped: (here) caught quickly
gulp: a large amount of something that you swallow at once
slurp: (here) noise made when eating
slobber: (here) sound when saliva drips from the mouth

**Peter:** Trust me! You must fly around the wolf, till he's sick and **dizzy**. And keep him near the bottom of the tree!

[*Bird flies round and round the wolf's head.*]

**Bird:** WHEEEEEEE!

**Wolf:** OI! Silly Bird. Go away. You're making me dizzy.

### Cross-curricular Corner

The food chain tells us how different animals eat and survive. Some animals, such as cats and wolves, are carnivores. They eat other animals. Some animals eat plants and nuts to survive. They are herbivores.

[*Peter makes a* **lasso** *out of the rope, and dangles it down until it slips over the wolf's tail.*]

**Narrator:** The wolf didn't see Peter... but he felt the lasso when it was pulled tight round his tail.

**Wolf:** OWW! What's that! Get off my tail!

[*Peter ties the end of the rope round the thick branch he and Cat are sitting on – still high in the tree.*]

**Peter:** Ha ha! I've got you, you big, bad wolf.

**Narrator:** Just as Peter had tied up the wolf, a hunter came out of the forest and pointed his gun at Bird up in the tree.

**Peter:** Don't shoot! Bird and I have caught the big, bad wolf.

**Hunter:** Amazing! Let's take him to the zoo.

dizzy: the feeling of losing balance and about to fall

lasso: a long rope with a loop at one end

**Scene 4: The Zoo**

**Narrator:** Peter led the way to the zoo, followed by the hunter with the wolf. Grandfather went too, with Cat. Overhead, Bird chirped merrily.

**Grandfather:** You're a brave boy, Peter. I'm not cross with you anymore.

**Bird:** Tweet, tweet. Peter is the bravest boy in the world.

**Narrator:** But what about Duck? If you listen very carefully, you'll hear Duck quacking inside the wolf. The wolf, in his hurry to eat her, had swallowed her whole.

**Duck:** [*very quietly*] QUACK! QUACK! QUACK!

### In a Nutshell

- **Who** Peter, Grandfather, Bird, Duck, Cat, Wolf, and Hunter
- **Where** The meadows near Grandfather's house
- **What** Peter planned to catch the wolf.
- **Why** The wolf pounced on all the animals and tried to eat them.
- **How** Peter made a lasso and Bird circled around the wolf. The wolf got dizzy, and Peter caught him.

### About the author

Diane Redmond is an author, television scriptwriter, and dramatist. Among her first children's books were the *Fireman Sam* titles. She has also written several plays for the Polka Theatre Company. She lives in England with her family and two dogs.

## Comprehension

**A. Fill in the blanks with words from the story.**

1. ________________ was angry that Peter was playing in the meadow.
2. ________________ went to the meadow to play with his animal friends.
3. ________________ climbed the tree to catch Bird.
4. The wolf caught ________________.
5. The hunter helped Peter to take the wolf to the ________________.
6. At the end of the story, Grandfather was ________________ with Peter anymore.

**B. Answer these questions.**

1. What happened when Peter went to the meadows?
2. What did Cat do? Was he Bird's friend? Why/Why not?
3. What did Peter see from his window?
4. How did Peter trap the wolf?
5. What was Grandfather's reaction when Peter caught the wolf?

## Life Skills and Values

bravery and kindness

21ST CENTURY Critical Thinking

1. Do you think Peter was a brave boy? Give an example to support your answer.
2. Though Peter was young, he wanted to save the wolf's life. He stopped the hunter from shooting the wolf. What does this show about Peter?

## Vocabulary

suffixes

A **suffix** is a group of letters added after a word to form a new word.

**Examples:** careful + *-ly* → **carefully**
*danger* + *-ous* → **dangerous**

ia **A. Fill in the blanks with words formed by adding suitable suffixes to the given words.**

1. The kingdom (king) prospered under the noble king's rule.
2. Everyone praised his ________________ (help) nature.
3. Peter's ________________ (kind) has saved many animals.

4. Vinay noticed a sudden ________________ (move) in the bush.
5. Robin Hood was a ________________ (fear) man who had many adventures.
6. Rini was trying her best to make her relatives feel ________________ (comfort).

character adjectives

Sometimes, **adjectives** tell us about some person's or animal's character.

**Examples:** Peter says, 'I'm going to catch the **big, bad** wolf.'
Wolf says, '**Silly** Bird.'

In these sentences, *big, bad*, and *silly* are adjectives of the character of the wolf and Bird.

**B. Underline the adjectives that describe the characters in the following sentences.**

1. My dog is lazy, but it is adorable.
2. The cruel man had many enemies.
3. The timid mouse squeaked in surprise.
4. The humble musician was surprised by the praise.
5. Many people couldn't solve the puzzle, but the clever boy could.

## Grammar

types of adverbs

Read these sentences.

Who's afraid of the big, bad wolf?' Peter asked **crossly**.

Duck waddled out of the pond and ran to the clump of trees **nearby**.

Peter and the animals planned to play in the meadow **tomorrow**.

**Language Booster**

Some words can be used both as adverbs and as adjectives.

*Example:*

This is a **hard** nut. (*adjective*)

She worked **hard** for her test. (*adverb*)

The words *crossly, nearby,* and *tomorrow* are **adverbs**. Adverbs tell us how, where, and when an action takes place.

In the first sentence, the word *crossly* describes how Peter asked the question.

In the second sentence, the word *nearby* describes where the clump of trees was.

In the third sentence, the word *tomorrow* tells us when Peter and the animals will play.

**A. Change the following adjectives to adverbs.**

1. happy ____________________
2. graceful ____________________
3. courageous ____________________
4. proud ____________________
5. brave ____________________
6. dangerous ____________________

**B. Underline the adverbs in these sentences.**

1. The children are playing outside.
2. This is my school. I like studying here.
3. People must speak softly in the library.
4. Piya visited her grandparents yesterday.
5. My mother will pick me up from school today.
6. Bina walked quickly to the bus stop as she was getting late.

### conjunctions: *because* and *so*

Read these sentences.

Grandfather was angry **because** Peter was in the meadow.
Duck saw the wolf, **so** she waddled out of the pond.

The words *because* and *so* act as joining words in these sentences and are called conjunctions.

**Conjunctions** are words which join words or groups of words together.

**because** — shows the reason behind something

**so** — shows the result of something

**C. Fill in the blanks with *because* or *so*.**

1. I don't want to eat __________ I am not hungry.
2. I didn't sleep well last night, __________ I am tired now.
3. Peter was not afraid of the animals __________ he is brave.
4. Sheela had a toothache, __________ she went to the dentist.
5. Rita started to exercise and eat healthy __________ she wanted to remain fit.

## Study Skills

### Spelling

words ending in *-er* and *-ar*

- The *-er* and *-ar* endings are both used to form words which are associated with people and what they do.
  **Examples:** zookeep**er** hunt**er** begg**ar** burgl**ar**
- The *-er* ending is also used in words which refer to a person or thing that has a particular form.
  **Examples:** two-wheel**er** skyscrap**er**
- The *-ar* ending is also found in some other common nouns.
  **Examples:** coll**ar** pill**ar**

**Complete the words correctly with *-er* or *-ar*.**

1. calend__
2. bik__
3. rid__
4. doll__
5. bank__
6. fill__
7. gramm__
8. design__
9. hang__
10. farm__
11. caterpill__
12. cell__

## Listening

listening for information

**Listen to a passage about a girl named Shreya and write whether these statements are true (T) or false (F).**

1. Shreya's mother is a teacher. ☐
2. Shreya has two brothers. ☐
3. Shreya's neighbour, Mr Singh, likes gardening. ☐
4. There are only peach trees in his garden. ☐
5. Mr Chandel owns the grocery shop. ☐
6. Shreya's father's best friend is Mr Jeevi. ☐
7. The families go to the riverside for a picnic. ☐
8. Shreya likes to do fishing. ☐

### Dictation

**You will now listen to a short passage about Vidya's visit to a farm and write it down. Each sentence will be repeated twice. Listen carefully and try not to make any spelling errors.**

## Speaking

asking for and giving advice

Peter gets Duck out of the wolf's stomach. Duck is hurt. Now, Peter wants to help Duck and he is asking for advice from Grandfather. Grandfather advises Peter on how they can help Duck. Sometimes, we give advice to our friends and family about what should be done in a particular situation. We also ask them for advice.

**Read this conversation in which Grandfather gives Peter some advice.**

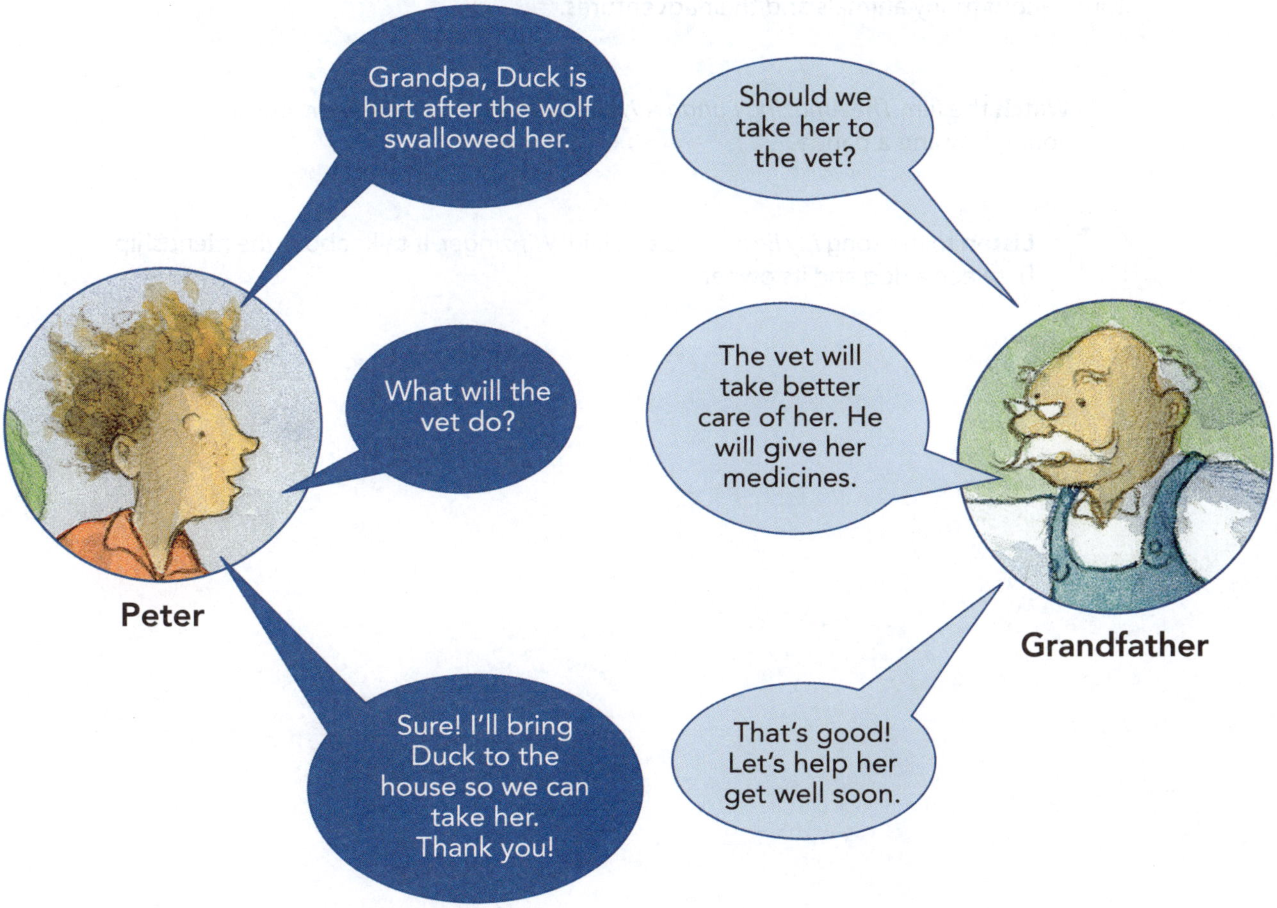


enacting the play

**Now, work in groups and enact the play that you read.**

## Writing

creative writing

**By the end of the play, Peter caught the wolf and saved the other animals of the meadow. He was also kind to the animals and did not let the hunter shoot them. Imagine that Peter has grown up and is going to visit the meadow again. How do you think he would react to the birds and animals in the meadow and forest?**

**You can start like this:**

*It has been ten years since Peter caught the big, bad wolf. The birds and animals in the forest have been living happily since then.*

## Explore More

**Read** the book *Animal Stories for Children* by Ruskin Bond. It is a collection of stories about funny animals and their adventures.

**Watch** the film *The Amazing Panda Adventure*. It shows the adventures of a young boy and a panda.

**Listen** to the song *My Best Friend* by Heidi Winzinger. It talks about the friendship between a dog and its owner.

# Project 2

**A. In the chapter *Around the World with a Chilli*, you read about the famous explorers Christopher Columbus and Vasco da Gama. Find out about any one of these famous explorers and make an information chart on them.**

21ST CENTURY Creativity

1. Marco Polo
2. Vasco da Gama
3. Ferdinand Magellan
4. Ibn Battuta

You can collect the following facts to make the information chart.

| Picture of the explorer | Where and when their expedition began | Mode of transport used (ship/caravan/ animals/on foot) | Interesting events that occurred during the trip | Places explored/ discovered | Your opinion about the explorer |
|---|---|---|---|---|---|
| | | | | | |

**B. You read about animal behaviour in the chapters *Trapped by a Tiger* and *Peter and the Wolf*. Now make a PowerPoint presentation on any animal/ bird around you, that can be found in parks or gardens near your home.**

You can include these points in your presentation.

- What does the creature look like? Does it have any special feature?
- Did you find something fascinating about it? Was its behaviour similar to or different from that of humans?
- Did you learn something from it?

UNIT VI

# Outer Space

## Warm-up

21st Century Critical Thinking

**A. Read the clues and find words related to space in the grid.**

| B | W | T | L | C | P | E | W | C | E | S | H | Z |
|---|---|---|---|---|---|---|---|---|---|---|---|---|
| P | Q | A | S | T | R | O | N | A | U | T | M | O |
| S | F | U | O | Z | B | X | X | D | X | J | R | B |
| B | S | M | A | T | E | L | E | S | C | O | P | E |
| Z | R | S | P | A | C | E | S | H | I | P | I | G |
| C | O | N | S | T | E | L | L | A | T | I | O | N |
| V | T | S | X | E | J | S | P | K | I | Q | P | T |
| W | X | C | P | L | A | N | E | T | T | X | O | R |

1. heavenly bodies that move around the sun: P __ __ __ __ T
2. a group of stars that forms a shape in the sky and has a name: C __ __ __ __ __ L __ __ __ __ __ N
3. an instrument with lenses through which distant objects appear closer: T __ __ __ __ __ __ __ E
4. someone who travels and works in a spacecraft: A __ __ __ O __ __ __ T
5. a vehicle that travels in space, carrying people: S __ __ __ __ __ __ __ P

**B. There are eight planets in our solar system, of which our Earth is the third. Read some interesting facts about six planets and guess their names.**

1. __________

2. __________

3. __________

4. __________

5. __________

6. __________

non-fiction

12

# Kalpana Chawla

Garima Kushwaha

### Curricular Goals

- develop a comprehensive range of vocabulary in various contexts
- develop fluency in reading and the ability to read with comprehension
- sustain effective communication skills for day-to-day interactions
- develop the ability to express themselves in writing

### Competencies

- can understand collocations
- can use different types of pronouns, and main and auxiliary verbs
- can say the different sounds of *th* and *gh*
- can express agreement and disagreement and write a few paragraphs about an incident

## Reading

**a** *Dr Kalpana Chawla was the first Indian-born woman astronaut to go into space. From a very early age, nothing meant more to her than to be able to live her dream of reaching the stars. Read on to find out more about Dr Kalpana Chawla.*

Growing up in Karnal, Haryana, Kalpana Chawla used to look up at the clear skies **speckled** with **constellations**. Often, she would spot a shooting star and wonder what they were. As an adult, she had the **privilege** of another view—looking down at Earth from the other side of the sky.

The **inhabitants** of that small town in Haryana kept their eyes peeled[1] for many years, watching for one of their own who had made the big leap into the **cosmos**—Kalpana, the first woman of Indian origin to fly into space.

Speaking of her experience, Kalpana said, 'I never truly thought of being the first or second someone. Or being a small-town girl. This is just something I wanted to do. It was very important for me to enjoy it. If you want to do something, what does it matter where you are ranked? Nor does being a woman make a difference[2].'

### Common idioms and proverbs

1. **keep your eyes peeled:** to watch very carefully
2. **make a difference:** have an effect

speckled: (here) covered with
constellations: groups of stars, forming patterns and having names
privilege: (here) advantage
inhabitants: people who live in a particular place
cosmos: the universe

In 1982, after **acquiring** a Bachelor of Science degree in Aeronautical Engineering from Punjab Engineering College, Kalpana left for the US. There, she earned a Master's degree from the University of Texas and a PhD from the University of Colorado, with a focus on **aeronautical engineering**.

When she got a break with NASA, she joined the Ames Research Centre. Only the brightest and fittest are selected for NASA's astronaut programme. She was then selected from an application pool of 2962 people, as one of 23 astronauts—of which only five were women—chosen to fly in the **Space Shuttle**.

Who was the first woman of Indian origin to fly into space?

## Cross-curricular Corner

The Space Shuttle Programme was the fourth human spaceflight programme carried out by NASA.

The Space Shuttle programme was one of the most **ambitious endeavours** in human history. Carrying a **crew** of seven to the limits of earth's atmosphere and back, it represented the **cutting-edge** technology of modern **spaceflight**. In November 1997, Kalpana went aboard the Space Shuttle Columbia as a mission specialist on flight STS-87, **tasked** with operating the **robotic arm**. The shuttle **orbited** Earth for over two weeks, carrying out several experiments.

Kalpana described her first trip into space to writer Warren E. Leary as 'Alice in Wonderland floating freely, and the Earth moving there below—as if I'd taken the "shrink-me" pill and seen the whole world go by in no time.' So, when she got another chance to fly in 2003, she grabbed the opportunity without **hesitation**. She was selected as the flight engineer and mission specialist for Columbia flight STS-107. When she described on radio the **awe-inspiring** moment of

acquiring: getting
aeronautical engineering: the branch of engineering concerned with the design, production, and maintenance of aircraft
space shuttle: a spacecraft designed to travel into space and back to earth several times
ambitious: (here) large scale idea or plan that needs a lot of work to be carried out successfully
endeavours: attempts to do something new or original
crew: people who work on a ship, aircraft, or spaceship
cutting-edge: the most advanced
spaceflight: a journey into or through space
tasked: assigned with a task or job to do
robotic arm: a machine with a mechanical arm
orbited: circled or went around
hesitation: an unwillingness to do something
awe-inspiring: amazing

stars reflecting in her eyes during a moving sunset, you could hear the joy in Kalpana's voice. 'In the **retina** of my eye, the whole Earth and the sky could be seen reflected,' said Kalpana.

She conducted 80 experiments in space and declared on the radio that her mission was complete. Along with the STS107 mission, Chawla completed her life's final mission. While she strapped herself in the shuttle to return to the Earth's atmosphere, space claimed her life.

Kalpana Chawla made **unconventional** choices for her time—from **opting** for **aerospace engineering** as a young student to becoming an astronaut as a woman. She always said that it was her **perseverance** and hard work that made her dreams come true.

Many places have been named in her honour, but one stands out: the Chawla Hill on the surface of Mars, which bears **immortal testimony** to this brave astronaut who gave her life for humanity's place amongst the stars.

retina: the area at the back of the eye that receives the image that you see and then sends the image to your brain

unconventional: unusual

opting: choosing

aerospace engineering: the branch of engineering that deals with the development and production of aircraft, rockets, space vehicles, and related equipment

perseverance: persistence, determination, or the quality of continuing with something even though it is difficult

immortal: (here) famous and likely to be remembered for a long time

testimony: (here) fact

## In a Nutshell

| | |
|---|---|
| **Who** | Kalpana Chawla |
| **What** | Visit to space |
| **When** | 1997, 2003 |
| **How** | Through hard work and perseverance |

## About the author

Garima Kushwaha is a scientist by profession. She is interested in inspiring young girls to become whatever they dream to be and writes about it. This story tells us that there is no set profession for girls.

## Comprehension

ia **A. Choose the correct options.**

1. Kalpana grew up in ______________.
   a. Karnal b. Kodaikanal c. Delhi
2. Kalpana was one of the ______________ female astronauts chosen to fly in the Space Shuttle.
   a. 23 b. 5 c. 10
3. Kalpana compared herself to ______________ when she spoke about her first trip to space.
   a. a child b. a bird c. Alice in Wonderland
4. She stayed in space for over ______________.
   a. a year b. two weeks c. a month
5. Chawla Hill is located on ______________.
   a. Mars b. Earth c. Jupiter

**B. Answer these questions.**

1. What was Kalpana's role in the first space mission?
2. What was special about the Ames Research Centre?
3. How does Kalpana describe the view of the Earth from space?
4. What did Kalpana do in space during her second mission?
5. How did Kalpana achieve her dreams?

## Life Skills and Values

everyday science

21ST CENTURY Critical Thinking

1. Why do space programmes choose the best astronauts?
2. Why do you think astronauts carry out experiments in space?

## Vocabulary

collocations

Read these sentences.

It was a **big leap** for Kalpana from a small city to NASA.
Kalpana Chawla made **unconventional choices**.

The words in bold usually go together. These are called **collocations**.

**Collocations** are pairs or sets of words that are commonly used together.

**Fill in the blanks with the correct options.**

1. She went out in the ______________ (heavy/big) rain.
2. There was a ______________ (loud/big) noise outside.
3. It was ______________ (amazing/freezing) cold last December.
4. The children should ______________ (make/do) their beds before they watch TV.
5. There was ______________ (heavy/large) traffic on the roads due to the sudden rain.
6. Aryan was ______________ (highly/extremely) happy to meet his friends after the vacation.

## Grammar

types of pronouns

Pronouns are words used in place of nouns. The pronouns *I, you, he, she, it, we, you,* and *they* refer to the speaker or the person spoken to. These are **personal pronouns.**

**Example:** Kalpana left for the US. There, **she** earned a master's degree from the University of Texas.

Personal pronouns refer to the subject or the object in a sentence.

Pronouns that are used as the subject in a sentence are called **subject pronouns.**

*I, you, he, she, it, we,* and *they* are subject pronouns.

Pronouns that are used as the object in a sentence, that is, after the verb, are called **object pronouns.**
*Me, you, him, her, it, us,* and *them* are object pronouns.

**Examples:** **She** would spot a shooting star. (*She*: subject pronoun)
It was very important for me to enjoy **it**. (*it*: object pronoun)

**Personal pronouns**
- Pronoun as subject — *I, you, he, she, it, we, they*
- Pronoun as object — *me, you, him, her, it, us, them*

Pronouns that show belonging are called **possessive pronouns**. These are *mine, ours, yours, theirs, hers,* and *his.*

**Example:** Kalpana received many awards. The medals are **hers**.

Pronouns that are used as objects of the verb but refer to the same person or thing as the subject are called **reflexive pronouns**. In such cases, the subject and the object in the sentence are the same.
*Myself, yourself, himself, herself, itself, ourselves, yourselves,* and *themselves* are reflexive pronouns.

**Example:** Kalpana motivated **herself**.

## ia A. Fill in the blanks with the correct subject or object pronouns.

1. We are going to the fair. Do ______________ want to come along?
2. My sister has a car. ______________ drives ______________ every day.
3. Mani brought a new pen to school. ______________ gave ______________ to his friend.
4. My friend and I enjoy our lessons. ______________ often learn ______________ together.
5. Bina had forgotten to bring her lunch. Raja offered ______________ from his lunch.
6. My cousin, Benny, is visiting ______________. ______________ wants to see these paintings.

## ia B. Choose the correct possessive or reflexive pronouns.

1. The fastest car in town is ______________ (his/himself).
2. You should do the work ______________ (yours/yourself).
3. Kalpana told ______________ (hers/herself) that she could do this.
4. Rita loves to do craftwork. She made these dolls ______________ (hers/herself).
5. The cat was alarmed and jumped into the bushes. It hurt ______________ (its/itself).
6. Many children participated in the contest. These entries are ______________ (theirs/themselves).

## main and auxiliary verbs

There are two types of verbs: main and auxiliary. **Main verbs** are those that show the action performed by the subject. They can be used by themselves in a sentence.

**Examples:** She **earned** a Master's degree.
Kalpana **described** her first trip into space.

**Auxiliary verbs** are helping verbs. They are placed before the main verb to show different tense forms as well as the person and number of the subject. The three main auxiliary verbs are *be*, *have*, and *do*.

Read these sentences.

| Auxiliary verb | Singular | Plural |
|---|---|---|
| *be* | I **am** going to the market. | They **are** going to the market. |
| *have* | Ronita **has** watched this film. | My brothers **have** watched this film. |
| *do* | He **does** not know the answer. | We **do** not know the answer. |

When forming questions, we place the auxiliary verb before the subject in the sentence.

**Example:** **Has** she returned the book? (*she* = subject)

**C. Fill in the blanks with suitable auxiliary verbs.**

1. I ________________ (has/am) going home now.
2. My father ________________ (had/did) washed the car last week.
3. They ________________ (are/have) going to Rajasthan this winter.
4. ________________ (Has/Does) Ravi know the answer to that question?
5. The students ________________ (does/have) completed their homework.
6. ________________ (Does/Have) you seen any constellation in a clear night sky?

## Study Skills

### Pronunciation Skills

different sounds of *th*

When a word has the letters *th* in it, we can pronounce it in two ways.

- with the soft *th* sound, as in *things*
- with the hard *th* sound, as in *these*

**A. Read the words aloud. Then, sort them in the correct columns.**

though thought this there with another thunder athlete father

| *th* as in *things* | *th* as in *these* |
|---|---|
| | |

words with *gh* sounds

When a word has the letters *gh* in it, we can pronounce it in these ways.

- with the *g* sound, as in *ghastly*
- with the *f* sound, as in *cough*
- silent, as in *through*

**B. Read the words aloud. Then, sort them in the correct columns.**

though enough weight ghost sigh yoghurt rough thought

| *gh* as in *ghastly* | *gh* as in *cough* | *gh* as in *through* |
|---|---|---|
| | | |

## Listening

listening to an interview and answering questions

**Listen to an interview and answer the following questions.**

1. Which planet are scientists talking about?
2. What is the other name of Mars?
3. Where will the volunteers live?
4. Name some activities that volunteers will do.
5. How does the project prepare the volunteers for survival?

### Dictation

**You will now listen to a short passage about the planet Mars and write it down. Each sentence will be repeated twice. Listen carefully and be careful not to make any spelling errors.**

## Speaking

expressing agreement or disagreement

**Do you think that working hard is important to succeed in life? Make two groups in the class and have a debate on this topic. You can use the following points.**

**Agree**

- We should work hard all the time.
- We should do every task to our best, one at a time.

**Disagree**

- We should work just to achieve our goals.
- We should do tasks according to how easily or quickly we can finish them.

**Useful words and phrases**

I agree that…
It's alright to…
I don't agree with you as…
I don't think that…
In my opinion…

## Writing

narrating an incident

**Imagine that you are the captain of a spaceship in space. You have just landed on Mars and you see some aliens. Describe what you saw in a few paragraphs. Also, draw what you saw based on your imagination. You can use the following points.**

- the people or animals around you and how they appear to you
- what the aliens say to you, and their reaction on seeing you
- a trip around the planet where you see various things different from Earth
- your thoughts and emotions as you describe this strange land

## Explore More

**Read** *Caroline's Comets*. This book by Emily Arnold McCully is about Caroline Herschel, the first woman to discover a comet.

poem

# 13 The Big Beyond

James Carter

**Curricular Goals**

- develop a comprehensive range of vocabulary in various contexts
- develop the ability to express themselves in writing

**Competencies**

- can use movement words and space-related phrases
- can write an anecdote

## Reading

**a** *Have you ever looked up at the sky and dreamt about flying to outer space? Read this poem to know about how humans have flown to the Moon and outer space in the past.*

Once upon a rocket a **countdown** has begun
From 10, 9, 8 to 7 and 6 to 5, 4, 3, 2, 1.

As early people watched the sky
They wished for wings so they could fly.

They dreamt up questions thick and fast…
How deep is space?
How far are stars?
Does planet Mars have life like ours?

And in those stars across the night
They drew some creatures formed of light,
From Crab to Lion – Bull to Bear
Such **starry beasts** were everywhere.

Through **telescopes** we found such things
As planets with their moons and rings.

We learnt we're of the **Milky Way**,
That stars are all so far away,

countdown: counting aloud of numbers in reverse order before an event, especially before a spacecraft is launched

starry beasts: (here) large animal-shaped formations of stars known as constellations

telescopes: instruments used to look at distant objects in the sky

Milky Way: the name of the galaxy that we live in

The force of space is **gravity**,
And there are endless **galaxies**.

Yet still, to fly was our great aim…
With kites, balloons, and **gliders**, planes.

And then in 1957 rockets **soared** towards the heavens.
Through the clouds up, up, and on out into…
THE BIG BEYOND!

UP! We sent beyond the night, to orbit Earth, a **satellite**.
UP! Went creatures: dogs and cats, monkeys, turtles, flies, and rats.
UP! In time went **astronauts**, space explorers, **cosmonauts**.

Then summer 1969 what a time for humankind!
A rocket known as **Saturn Five**
With smoke and flames burst into life.
And now in front of their TVs
The whole world watched excitedly.

What great adventure happened next?
Upon the Moon two men took steps!
And on that world so strange, so new
They left a flag,
Some footprints too.

Since then, we've been up many times
We've walked in space, launched satellites.
And to the planets spacecraft **roam**
Sending information home.

### Cross-curricular Corner

Sputnik 1 was the first artificial satellite to orbit the Earth from the Soviet Union.

Next, animals were sent to orbit the Earth followed by Russian cosmonaut, Yuri Gagarin in 1961.

On 21 July 1969, American astronauts Neil Armstrong and Edwin 'Buzz' Aldrin landed on the moon.

On 23 August 2023, India successfully landed on the surface of the moon in its third moon mission called Chandrayaan-3.

**gravity:** (here) the force of attraction that keeps all the planets in place
**galaxies:** large groups of stars and planets
**gliders:** aircraft without engines, which fly by floating on air currents
**soared:** (here) went quickly up into the air
**satellite:** (here) the moon
**astronauts:** persons who travel to space
**cosmonauts:** astronauts from the former Soviet Union
**Saturn Five:** a rocket built to send people to the moon
**roam:** to wander or go

To Mars, our neighbour, we've sent more –
**Probes** with which we could explore.
**Crafts** to land to test the air,
To sample soil, to check what's there.

New rockets, rockets every year
Will head out through the atmosphere.
We'll need an astronaut (or two)
So, what do you think?
Could it be YOU?

probes: spacecrafts that travel into space with no people in it, usually to study the planets and send information about them back to earth

crafts: (here) spacecrafts

### In a Nutshell

**What** Space travel

**When** Since people started watching the sky

**Why** Because people are curious about space

**How** Using rockets and spacecraft

**Who** Astronauts and cosmonauts

### About the poet

James Carter is an award-winning children's poet, who lives in the UK. He travels all over the UK to promote poetry through performances and workshops. *Outstanding* and *Best Visitor We've Ever Had* are some of his poems.

## Understanding the Poem

**A. Complete the sentences with words and phrases from the poem.**

1. Early people wished for ________________ so they could fly.
2. We found planets and their moons using ________________.
3. The first rockets were launched in ________________.
4. ________________ was the rocket launched in 1969.
5. The Earth and the Sun are in the ________________.
6. We will need more ________________ in future.

**B. Read the lines and answer the questions.**

1. *And in those stars across the night*
   *They drew some creatures formed of light,*
   a. What does the poet mean by 'creatures'?
   b. Which creatures did 'they' draw?
   c. Who does the poet refer to as 'they'?

2. *Then summer 1969 what a time for humankind!*
*A rocket known as Saturn Five*
*With smoke and flames burst into life.*

   a. Why was the summer of 1969 an important time for humankind?
   b. What was special about the rocket known as Saturn Five?
   c. What does 'With smoke and flames burst into life' mean?

3. *Crafts to land to test the air,*
*To sample soil, to check what's there.*

   a. Where do these craft(s) land?
   b. Why do they need to test the air?
   c. What do the craft(s) do with the soil?

## Life Skills and Values

being aware

21ST CENTURY Critical Thinking

1. Space travel is exciting, but also frightening. If you were an astronaut, how would you feel about being in space?
2. Why do you think space travel is important for humankind?

## Vocabulary

movement words

ia **A. This poem uses various movement words like *fly, roam,* and *walk*. Fill in the circles with the correct movement words of each type.**

tiptoe flutter stroll jog travel wander flap glide march

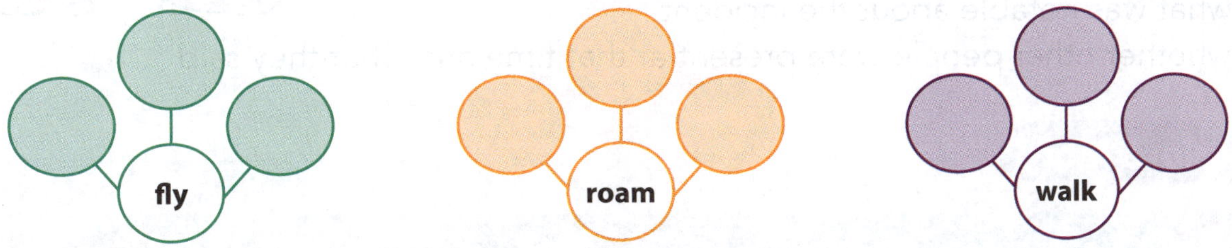


**B. Fill in the blanks with words from the previous exercise. You may have to change the tense of some words.**

1. The butterfly ____________ its wings.
2. Don't ____________ around the busy fair.
3. Rina saw the eagle ____________ effortlessly.
4. Every morning my brother and I ____________ in the park.
5. I ____________ into the room not wanting to wake my brother up.

space-related phrases

**ia C. The poem you just read is about the history of space travel. Match the 'space' phrases with their meanings.**

| Phrase | Meaning |
|---|---|
| 1. watch this space | a. a short break taken between two activities |
| 2. breathing space | b. during a period of time |
| 3. stare into space | c. used to show that more information about something will be given later |
| 4. in the space of | d. to be completely useless |
| 5. a waste of space | e. to fill up space |
| 6. take up space | f. look straight at front, without seeing anything in particular |

## Activity

writing an anecdote

21ST CENTURY Creativity

An **anecdote** is a short amusing story about something that happened.

**Write an anecdote about something funny that happened when you went on vacation.**

**You can include the following points.**

- what the incident was
- when and where it happened
- why you found it funny
- what was notable about the incident
- whether other people were present at that time and what they said

## Explore More

**Read** the poem *Pluto's not a Planet Anymore* by Jeff Modak. It is about the dwarf planet, Pluto, once counted as the ninth planet in our solar system.

**Watch** the film *Fly Me to the Moon*. It is about Nat who wants to reach the moon and enters a rocket without permission.

**Listen** to *Marlow's Going to Space* by Peanut Butter Jams. It is a song about space travel.

UNIT VII

# Different but Same

## Warm-up

**A. Look at the names and descriptions of some well-known people who are differently abled. Guess who they are and match the names with the descriptions.**

| Name | Description |
|---|---|
| 1. Ludwig van Beethoven | a. He could not hear properly and was unable to read until the age of eleven. He invented the electric light bulb that could be used inside homes. |
| 2. Sudha Chandran | b. She lost her eyesight and her ability to hear as a child. But she learnt to read with the help of her teacher, Anne Sullivan. |
| 3. Thomas Alva Edison | c. She lost a leg in an accident, but she went on to become a well-known dancer and actress. |
| 4. Helen Keller | d. He was a brilliant pianist and musician, who started losing his hearing from the age of 30.<br>He composed some of his best musical pieces while he was deaf. |

**B. Sign language is a method of communication used by people who are unable to speak or hear. In sign language, certain hand movements often stand for letters or words. Look at the pictures and guess the words they stand for, choosing from the ones given. Write them under the correct pictures.**

love stop afraid sorry sad angry

1. ________ 2. ________ 3. ________ 4. ________ 5. ________ 6. ________

mystery

# 14 Earrings for Nina

Asha Nehemiah

### Curricular Goals

- develop a comprehensive range of vocabulary in various contexts
- develop fluency in reading and the ability to read with comprehension
- sustain effective communication skills for day-to-day interactions
- develop the ability to express themselves in writing

→

### Competencies

- can understand anagrams and order of adjectives in a sentence
- can use the degrees of comparison of adjectives, and apostrophe for contractions and possessions
- can say the soft and hard *c* sounds
- can speak by using degrees of comparison and describe an event in a paragraph

## Reading

**a** *What would you do if you found yourself in the middle of a robbery? Would you try to save others or try to save yourself? Read the story of a brave young girl who used her special ability to solve a crime.*

SUSTAINABLE DEVELOPMENT GOALS 10 REDUCED INEQUALITIES

'Which pair of earrings do you like, Nina? **Dangling** silver parrots or these rose-shaped ones?' Rekha asked her sister. Rekha always made sure that her younger sister could watch her face as she spoke.

The two sisters had come with their mother to the jewellery store.

Why was Nina angry?

'I don't want earrings. Please leave me alone!' replied Nina.

'But Grandma sent money for both of us to buy earrings for our birthdays,' Rekha said. Nina's tenth birthday was only a few days away.

'But I don't want earrings. And I hate it when people stare at me as if I've run away from the zoo!' Nina said angrily.

'People will only stare at you if you keep **snapping** and **snarling**,' replied Rekha. She growled loudly like a tiger[1]. Nina **broke into** a laugh.

**Literary term**

1. This is a **simile**. Rekha made a sound as loud and deep as that of a tiger's growl.

Rekha's heart lifted with joy. Nina did not laugh much these days. Two years ago, Nina had got a dangerous brain fever. She got better, but could not hear anymore.

dangling: hanging
snapping: speaking irritably
snarling: speaking angrily
broke into: (here) started laughing

Nina had joined a special school where she learned to 'hear' what people said by watching their lips move. After months of training, Nina went back to her old school. But it was hard for her to understand what her teachers said. She felt sad when she could not take part in her favourite music programmes. The look of **pity** she saw in the eyes of her friends was the hardest for her. One day, Nina just stopped going to school.

Now, whenever her parents talked about school, she **burst into tears**.

'Come on, Nina,' Rekha asked her now. 'Don't buy earrings. But come and help me choose a pair.'

The store was famous for its diamond jewellery. They were always kept locked in glass cabinets. Only the store manager could unlock them for customers. There were security cameras everywhere. The counter where Nina and Rekha were standing was right next to the diamond section. Nina watched without interest as the salesman laid out many velvet-lined trays of beautiful earrings. A pair of beautiful dolphin-shaped earrings caught her eye[2].

**Common idioms and proverbs**

2. **catch somebody's eye:** to catch somebody's attention
3. **be green with envy:** be very jealous

'Aren't these cute?' she asked, holding up an earring with a smile.

Rekha nodded. 'It is just the thing to turn all your friends in school green with envy[3]!'

'Oh no, *didi*,' Nina shot back, 'I don't want to buy them. I'm not going back to school.'

The salesman looked at her mother. He pointed to Nina, then to his ear and shook his palm and asked, 'Can't the child hear?'

Nina was very upset and would not look at the earrings after that. She waited for her mother and sister to finish shopping.

Suddenly, she noticed two men, guns in hand, face covered with black masks, **burst into** the room.

What did Nina notice?

Robbers!

pity: the feeling of sorry for others' troubles

burst into tears: started crying

burst into: (here) broke into

One masked man **grabbed** the security guard. The other walked into the diamond section.

**Chaos** broke out! People screamed and ran in confusion.

The manager reached for the telephone in **panic**, when the robber fired a shot. The manager **clutched** his hand and cried out in pain. He was forced to unlock the cabinets. In less than a few minutes, the masked men had robbed the store and left.

Soon after, policemen arrived at the store.

'Let's leave at once, *ma*,' Rekha said, her voice shaking in fear.

But the police inspector stopped them. 'I'm sorry, but we have to take your **statements**. You are **witnesses** to a most daring robbery.'

Why did the inspector stop Nina's family from leaving the store?

Mrs Verma agreed to stay. 'But please don't trouble my younger daughter. She is scared of strangers,' she added.

'I'm not scared of anybody,' Nina said in a clear, **confident** voice. 'Sir, I think I can tell you more about this robbery than anyone else here.'

'What nonsense!' Mrs Verma said nervously, 'You don't have to do this.'

'I must,' came the reply, 'I'm the only one who could "hear" what was happening inside that glass room.'

The inspector led the three of them to one side.

Nina pointed to the manager who was having his hand bandaged by one of the policemen and said, 'He warned the robber not to shoot the glass cabinets, because it would set off the alarm.'

The manager looked shocked.

**Cross-curricular Corner**

Lip reading is used by people who cannot hear. Lip readers watch the movements of one's mouth, tongue and teeth to understand what they are saying.

'What rubbish!' he said, **scornfully**, 'That room is **sound-proof**!'

'But I can hear through **bullet-proof** glass in a very special way,' said Nina calmly. 'By watching people move their lips!'

'Inspector, this girl is lying,' the manager said angrily. 'Would the robbers have shot me if I was in league with[4] them?'

'Yes, that surprised you, didn't it?' Nina replied. 'You shouted at the masked man saying that they had agreed not to hurt you!'

**Common idioms and proverbs**

4. **in league with:** making secret plans (with somebody)

grabbed: took hold of roughly
chaos: a state of confusion
panic: a sudden feeling of great fear
clutched: held tightly
statements: official accounts of events
witnesses: people who have seen an event happen
confident: feeling sure about oneself
scornfully: showing no respect
sound proof: that does not allow sound to pass through
bullet proof: made of strong material that cannot be damaged with bullets

The manager looked scared now. 'Inspector, you're not going to believe this deaf girl, are you?'

'Inspector,' Nina continued, 'Please take the recorded tape from the store's video camera to my special school. The principal can watch it and tell you what the manager said.'

The manager started shouting loudly as the inspector ordered his men to take him away to the police station for questioning.

'You were amazing, my dear!' the inspector said, shaking Nina's hand. 'This case could only be solved because of you and your special **abilities**!'

He gave Nina a 'thumbs up' sign.

When the three of them walked out of the store, Rekha said with a **shudder**, 'I will never set foot in this store again!'

'Well, if you don't come with me,' said Nina, 'I'll just have to come on my own tomorrow.'

'Why do you want to come again tomorrow?' asked Rekha and Mrs Verma, **astonished**.

'To buy myself those dolphin-shaped earrings!' said Nina, cheerfully.

abilities: qualities

astonished: surprised

shudder: a shaking movement caused by fear

## In a Nutshell

| | |
|---|---|
| Who | Nina, a brave young girl |
| What | She helped solve a robbery. |
| Where | In a jewellery store |
| When | While shopping for earrings |
| How | By lip-reading an important conversation |

### About the author

Asha Nehemiah (b. 1958) is a children's author whose stories are humorous and filled with mystery. These have been translated into Tamil, Bengali, Assamese, and Hindi. *The Mystery of the Secret Hair Formula* and *Zigzag and Other Stories* are some of the books written by her.

## Comprehension

**A. Write whether the following statements are true (T) or false (F). Write the false statements correctly in your notebook.**

1. Nina and Rekha were friends. ☐
2. Nina could not hear after getting a brain fever. ☐

3. Nina could 'hear' people by watching their lips move. ☐
4. Rekha was the first one to notice the masked men enter the jewellery store. ☐
5. The robbers shot the manager. ☐
6. The manager was not involved in the robbery. ☐

## B. Answer these questions.

1. What did Rekha make sure of while talking to Nina?
2. Which school did Nina join after she lost her hearing? What did she learn there?
3. Why did Nina get upset when she was at the store?
4. Why didn't Nina want to go back to her old school?
5. What did the robbers do immediately after entering the store?
6. How did Nina help the police?
7. Why did Nina want to come back to the store?

## Life Skills and Values

being sensitive

21ST CENTURY Critical Thinking

1. Why do you think people stared at Nina? Do you think they were right in doing so?
2. Do you think Nina was an intelligent girl? Give reasons for your answer.

## Vocabulary

anagrams

An **anagram** is a play on words created by rearranging the letters of the original word to make a new word or phrase.

**Examples:** **stare → tears** **lips → slip**

### Write the anagrams of these words using the clues.

1. **arm** → ____ram____ (a male sheep)
2. **tea** → ____________ (past tense of eat)
3. **spelt** → ____________ (past tense of sleep)
4. **below** → ____________ (a part of our body)
5. **cars** → ____________ (a mark from an injury)
6. **bread** → ____________ (hair on a man's face)
7. **nap** → ____________ (something you cook in)
8. **horse** → ____________ (a place where land meets sea)

**Grammar** order of adjectives

When there are two or more adjectives in a sentence, we maintain the following order.

quantity/number → quality/opinion → size → age → shape → colour → origin → material

**Examples:**

Do you like the earrings with **dangling** (*quality*) **silver** (*material*) parrots, or these rose-shaped ones?

My mother bought **three** (*number*) **big,** (*size*) **brown,** (*colour*) **wooden** (*material*) chairs from the furniture shop.

ia **A. Fill in the blanks with the correct options.**

1. I bought a pair of ________________ dresses.
   a. black, cotton b. cotton, black
2. Ravi's brother is a ________________ boy.
   a. gentle, young b. young, gentle
3. Shreya's grandparents lived in an ________________ bungalow.
   a. British, big, old b. old, big, British
4. Arya has a ________________ doll's house.
   a. lovely, old, wooden b. wooden, old, lovely
5. Look at that ________________ car.
   a. beautiful, small, yellow b. yellow, small, beautiful
6. My mother is baking a ________________ cake.
   a. chocolate, round, delicious b. delicious, round, chocolate

adjectives: degrees of comparison

Look at these sentences.

These earrings are **pretty**.
The parrot earrings are **prettier** than the rose-shaped ones.
The dolphin-shaped earrings are the **prettiest**.

The words *pretty*, *prettier*, and *prettiest* are adjectives. We use adjectives to compare a particular quality between people and things.

The word *pretty* describes the earrings. It is in the **positive degree**.

In the second sentence, two types of earrings are being compared using the adjective *prettier*. It is in the **comparative degree**.

In the third sentence, more than two earrings are being compared. It is in the **superlative degree**. It shows that the dolphin-shaped earrings are the *prettiest* of the three.

Look at this table to see how the degrees of comparison are formed.

| Positive | Comparative | Superlative |
|---|---|---|
| tall | taller (add *-er*) | tallest (add *-est*) |
| careful | more careful (add *more*) | most careful (add *most*) |
| little | less (form changes completely) | least (form changes completely) |

ia **B. Fill in the blanks with the correct degrees of comparison.**

1. I feel Manali is ______________ (beautiful) than Shimla.
2. Priya's school bag is ______________ (heavy) than mine.
3. Rajeshwari is the ______________ (smart) girl in the class.
4. Pineapples are usually ______________ (sweet) than oranges.
5. This is the ______________ (old) castle in the United Kingdom.
6. I ate ______________ (much) rice than Manya, but Tanya ate the ______________ (little) among us.

## apostrophe for contractions

You know that a contraction is a word formed by joining two or more words and leaving out some letters. We use an apostrophe (') in contractions to show where the letters have been dropped.

Look at some common contractions.

**Contractions**

- that is → *that's*; he is → *he's*
- you are → *you're*; they are → *they're*
- do not → *don't*; will not → *won't*
- you will → *you'll*; I will → *I'll*
- I have → *I've*; we have → *we've*
- she had → *she'd*; he would → *he'd*

**C. Rewrite the sentences using suitable contractions.**

1. You are late.
2. What is the time?
3. She will come tomorrow.
4. They are not coming with us.
5. We have been waiting for you.
6. I do not know who broke the vase.

apostrophe to show possession

An **apostrophe (')** is used to show that someone or something belongs or relates to someone or something else.

We add an apostrophe *s ('s)* at the end of singular words or personal names.
**Examples:** store**'s** video, Rekha**'s** heart

We add an apostrophe *s ('s)* at the end of plurals that do not end in *s*.
**Examples:** children**'s** grandmother, men**'s** shirts

We can add either an apostrophe *(')* or an apostrophe *s ('s)* with names that already end in *s*.
**Examples:** James**'** lantern, Tejas**'** pencil

We use only an apostrophe *(')* with plurals that already end in *s*.
**Examples:** the girls**'** mother, the robbers**'** masks

**D. Fill in the blanks with the correct options.**

1. The ________________ (girls/girls') mother was frightened.
2. ________________ (Charles'/Charle's) house is close to mine.
3. Nina watched the ________________ (men's/mens') lips while they spoke.
4. Nina was happy with the ________________ (inspector's/ inspectors) praise.
5. My ________________ (grandparents'/grandparents) house is next to the beach.
6. She went to the store to buy her ________________ (sisters/sister's) present.

## Study Skills

### Pronunciation

soft and hard *c* sounds

**Listen to these words and repeat them.**

| | |
|---|---|
| cat | ice |
| coat | cell |
| cut | palace |

The letter *c* has a soft sound, as in *palace* and a hard sound, as in *cat*.

**Help Jeremy separate the words on the basis of their pronunciation, and put them in the right basket.**

## Listening

listening to a passage and sequencing

**Listen to a passage about Nikita's visit to a blind school and number the sentences in the order of events.**

- ☐ During lunchtime, we shared a hearty meal together.
- ☐ The first thing we saw was students using Braille in the classrooms.
- ☐ We said our goodbyes and promised to stay in touch with our new friends.
- ☐ Last Saturday, our class went on a day trip to a blind school with our teachers.
- ☐ The students were reading from a book which had pages with such letters.
- ☐ We also joined in and made a few handicrafts with them.
- ☐ I had made a new friend called Reshma and we exchanged phone numbers.
- ☐ In the crafts room, we saw children knitting wool, making clay toys and straw baskets.

## Speaking

speaking by using degrees of comparison

**In the story, Nina was *younger* than her sister but the *bravest* and *most confident* of all at the jewellery store. Did you notice the adjectives *younger*, *bravest*, and *most confident*? They are in different degrees of comparison. Now, talk about your family for half a minute, using degrees of comparison of adjectives.**

**You can use the following points.**

- the number of people in your family
- the tallest/shortest member
- any member in the family younger than you
- the most/least talkative member

## Writing

describing an event

**Imagine that you are Nina and you see the robbers enter the store. Write a paragraph describing the events which happen afterwards, in your own words. Mention the emotions that you felt at that time.**

**You can start like this:**

Last Saturday, I had gone to a jewellery store with my mother and my sister. We were looking at earrings when I saw two masked men enter the store…

**Useful words and phrases**

shocked, curious, frightened, happy, nervous, puzzled

## Explore More

**Read** the story *Granny's Sari* by Asha Nehemiah. It describes Granny and Anu's search for Granny's favourite sari which has been blown away.

**Watch** the short film *The Present*. It is about a special gift that a differently abled boy gets from his mother.

**Listen** to the song *Do You See Me as an Equal?* By Jeff Moyer. It talks about accepting the differently abled as they are and appreciating their strengths.

15 poem

# I See What You Miss

Barbara Bodine

### Curricular Goals

- develop a comprehensive range of vocabulary in various contexts
- develop the ability to express themselves in writing

### Competencies

- can use words related to the senses
- can write a poem

## Reading

**a** *Each of us sees the world differently. Read this poem about a person who cannot see but has a very strong sense of hearing and touch which she uses to know and understand the world around her.*

SUSTAINABLE DEVELOPMENT GOALS 10 REDUCED INEQUALITIES

I may not see the way you do
With eyes so bright and quick
But I know where flowers abound
And where the grass grows thick

I know if you are **kinda** little
And I know if you are tall
Oh I can see so many things
You may not see at all.

I use my ears and hands for eyes
And make them see for me
I **listen hard** and gently touch
And thus it is I see

I wonder if God had a reason
For making me like this,
**Perhaps** he meant for me to see
What other people miss!

kinda: kind of, when said informally
listen hard: (here) to listen carefully
perhaps: possibly

### Cross-curricular Corner

Braille is a series of raised dots that can be read with the fingers by people who are blind or whose eyesight is too poor to read printed material. Braille is not a language, but a code by which languages such as English or Spanish may be written and read.

### In a Nutshell

**Who** A young girl

**What** She uses her ears and hands to feel things around her.

**Why** She is visually impaired.

**How** By listening carefully and touching gently

### About the poet

Barbara Bodine wrote poetry for children. Her poetry speaks about difficult situations and how to look beyond a difficulty and overcome problems.

## Understanding the Poem

### A. Read the lines and answer the questions.

1. *I may not see the way you do*
   *With eyes so bright and quick*
   a. What do you understand by the first line?
   b. Whose 'eyes' is the poet talking about?
   c. How does the poet describe the 'eyes'?
2. *Oh I can see so many things*
   *You may not see at all.*
   a. What do you understand by the first line?
   b. What are the 'many things' that the poet can see?
   c. Who is 'you' in the second line and why won't they see them at all?
3. *Perhaps he meant for me to see*
   *What other people miss!*
   a. Who is 'he' in these lines?
   b. What is the poet wondering about?
   c. What do these lines say about the poet? Is she a hopeful person?

### B. Answer these questions.

1. In the first stanza, what are the two things the poet can notice?
2. In the second stanza, what can the poet observe which the others might have missed?
3. What does the poet use instead of eyes?
4. How does the poet 'see' with the other two senses?
5. How does the poet feel about her gifts?

## Life Skills and Values

gratitude and sensitivity

1. Do you think we should all be grateful for being able to see? Why?
2. Does the poet feel blessed about her special strengths? Give reasons for your answer.

## Vocabulary

words related to the senses

**We have five senses—sight, hearing, smell, taste, and touch. Write these words related to the senses in the correct columns.**

sweet dirty clean sour
bang boom fragrant smelly
rotten fresh splash bitter big
tasty salty wet cold rough
smooth crash

| sight | hearing | smell | taste | touch |
|---|---|---|---|---|
| | | | | |

**Now make sentences of your own with any two words for each sense.**

**Activity**

writing a poem

21ST CENTURY Creativity

**Read this poem.**

| | |
|---|---|
| Winter | *(name of the season)* |
| Fog everywhere | *(what you see)* |
| Smell of burning wood | *(what you smell)* |
| Falling of raindrops | *(what you hear)* |
| Taste of sweet hot chocolate | *(what you taste)* |
| Snuggling in the warm, soft quilts | *(what you touch)* |
| Winter | *(name of the season)* |

**Write a poem about your favourite season or food item, referring to each of the five senses, as in the poem you have just read. Use the given structure to write your poem.**

**Useful words and phrases**

hot - lot, cream - dream, drops - mops, snow - blow

**Explore More**

**Read** the story *Happy in Our Skin* by Fran Manushkin. It is about how people look different but are the same.

**Watch** the film *Red Like the Sky*. It is about a boy who is nearly sightless. He goes to a school for visually impaired children and discovers various ways to express himself.

# UNIT VIII Humour

## Warm-up

Mindfulness Activity
solving riddles/puzzles

Critical Thinking

**A. Work in pairs. Solve the riddles.**

1. What has a neck but no head? ____________
2. What is at the end of a rainbow? ____________
3. What has hands but cannot clap? ____________
4. What must be broken before you can use it? ____________
5. What gets wetter and wetter the more it dries? ____________
6. What belongs to you but is used mostly by others? ____________
7. I'm tall when I'm young and I'm short when I'm old. Who am I? ____________
8. I start with the letter T, I am filled with T and I end in T. Who am I? ____________

**B. Draw a combination of two or three animals and create a new animal of your own. It can be a horse with an elephant's trunk or a dog with a crocodile's tail. Give it a name and explain it briefly. Don't forget to colour the animal with your imagination.**

Creativity

short story

# 16 Lion on the Loose

Paro Anand

## Curricular Goals

- develop a comprehensive range of vocabulary in various contexts
- develop fluency in reading and the ability to read with comprehension
- sustain effective communication skills for day-to-day interactions
- develop the ability to express themselves in writing

## Competencies

- can understand phrasal verbs and spell words ending with *-sion*, *-cian*, and *-tion*
- can use simple future tense and identify different types of sentences
- can talk about a book and write a dialogue

## Reading

**a** *A lion in the zoo decided to step out and explore the city. Did he succeed? Read on to find out.*

Once it started raining, it just wouldn't stop. The sky wept great tears in an endless stream[1] until the clouds had entered everyone's hearts and made them feel as grey and weepy as the weather[2]. But still it rained on and on.

Everyone stayed at home, **gloomy** and bored. 'I wish we could DO something,' **moaned** Geeti, 'Nothing exciting ever happens to us,' said Vikki.

Mummy wouldn't let them go out but she tried to cheer them up by baking a cake. The children helped too. The cake was yummy and they ate it hot. The rest they covered and left on the table.

'I wonder what the animals and birds do?' asked Geeti thoughtfully.

'They must be **cooped up** in their cages.'

'No, silly, I mean the wild ones. The tigers in the jungles, the birds on trees; what do they do in all this rain?'

### Literary terms

1. This is an example of **personification**. The sky is being imagined as a person who is crying.
2. This is an example of **simile**. The people are being compared to the weather.

gloomy: (here) unhappy
moaned: made a low sound, when unhappy
cooped up: made to stay inside a building or in a small place and therefore unhappy

'At least they're free. Think of the animals in the zoo. How awful for them.'

And it was true. The animals in the zoo were worried and **irritable**. The wet weather was terrible for the creatures, big and small.

The more it rained, the more everything filled up with water. The **moat** around the lion's **enclosure** filled up too. The lion watched. He was an old fellow, who had never been out of the enclosure. He had never seen anything like this before. As the water **lapped** against the sides of the moat **temptingly**, the old fellow decided to make a go for it[3]. He sniffed here, and he sniffed there. He put one paw delicately into the water and then, with one big breath, he jumped right in.

At first he sank. Then he **panicked**. He thought for one awful moment that he was going to die. But he didn't. His mighty head popped up and he **paddled** along until he could feel the wall just under his chin. Putting his big paws onto the wall, he **heaved** himself up. And then he was out. Out and free. Free to walk around the world, just as he had seen hundreds of people do. Now he, the mighty king, was going to have the adventure of a lifetime.

## Common idioms and phrases

3. **make a go for something:** to take an action immediately

No one saw him, for it was night and all the zookeepers were fast asleep. Lion walked out, king of everything he saw. Softly, softly, he crept on **padded feet** to the enclosure next to him. He grinned at the bear, who woke up with a **start**.

Who were fast asleep when Lion passed by them?

He looked in at all the cages and thought how wonderful it was to be free. Then he had an idea. He was going to be really free. What was the point of freedom if he was still within the four walls of the zoo? So, asking the way at every cage he passed, Lion reached the main gate.

irritable: easily annoyed
moat: a deep ditch dug around a place and filled with water
enclosure: an area of land surrounded by a wall or fence and used for a particular purpose
lapped: (here) touched the sides gently
temptingly: in a way that is attractive or inviting
panicked: suddenly felt anxious or afraid
paddled: (here) walked in shallow water
heaved: (here) lifted or pulled
padded feet: feet of animals with soft covering for comfort and protection
start: (here) a slight involuntary movement of the body because of surprise or fear

He could smell a human. He carefully **peered** into the ticket booth. Sure enough, the guard sat there. Lion was a clever old fellow and knew that the guard wouldn't let him just walk out. So, he waited and watched. The guard didn't move. He snored gently. When Lion was sure that the man was fast asleep, he **padded** his way past him gently.

'Hmmm… humph…' said the guard in his sleep. Lion almost roared in fright. But he didn't, he waited quietly until he was sure that all was safe. And then he was FREE! Really free, for the very first time in his life.

What did the little child say to his father?

He walked around, looking with wonder at the big, black, wet roads. He stared up at the high buildings and he sniffed at people **huddled up**, asleep in the driest corners they could find. One little child peeped out of his thin blanket and saw him. 'Papa,' he whispered, 'there's a lion on the loose!' 'Yes, yes,' said his Papa sleepily, 'He'll go away; now get back to sleep.'

And Lion went on. This was the longest walk that he had ever had. He was in the bazaar now. But of course, everyone was fast asleep. He peered into shop windows, **fascinated** by the glittering things that shone there.

He walked on and on. On and on. Until he was one very wet, hungry, and tired lion. He now suddenly caught the smell of freshly baked cake. He'd never smelled anything so invitingly warm or warmly inviting. Sniff! Sniff! Sniff! He found the window to Geeti and Vikki's room open. Quickly, quietly, he jumped right in. He saw the children asleep in their soft, warm beds. And he felt like getting in with them. But first to find out where that delicious smell was coming from. Sniff! Sniff! Sniff!

Of course, with his sharp lion's nose, he found the cake. And with his sharp lion's teeth, he quickly gulped it down. It was delicious. Not like the smelly raw meat he usually got.

And now, to bed. Slipping back into the children's room, Lion tried to get into Vikki's bed.

peered: looked very hard to see clearly
padded: walked with quick, light, and quiet steps
huddled up: (here) slept very close together
fascinated: found something very interesting

But it was too small for one big lion. So, he crawled under the bed and found it wonderfully cosy and just right for one big lion. Soon he was fast asleep.

Next morning, Mummy woke up to find the cake missing.

'Did you eat the cake?'

'No, Mummy.'

'Then who could it have been?'

'It must have been the lion!' said Geeti.

'What lion? Geeti, don't be silly.'

'She's not being silly' said Vikki.

'There's a lion under my bed!'

'What?' shouted Mummy loudly. And she rushed right away to look for the lion under her daughter's bed.

She looked, but there was no lion there. 'Oh children,' she said crossly, 'You gave me a fright. Of course, there's no lion there.'

Where did Lion take a snooze?

## Cross-curricular Corner

Lions are not known for being strong swimmers, and they generally avoid bodies of water, especially during heavy floods. They are not adapted to aquatic life like some other big cats, such as tigers, which are known to be strong swimmers.

'But there was, Mummy,' **protested** the children. 'Look, there are lion paw prints on the carpet.'

'And a big wet patch on our beds.'

'And lion hair on my sheet!'

Mummy had to believe them then, but try as they might, they couldn't find the lion any more. And do you know why? The lion had a good **snooze** and decided to get back to his cage before there was any **fuss**. So, he had slipped away at dawn and no one saw him going. He slipped past the guard who still lay asleep and swam back into his cage. What an adventure it had been! But he was glad to be home.

protested: argued against something because you think it is wrong

snooze: a short sleep

fuss: unnecessary nervous or excited behaviour

As soon as the rain stopped, Geeti and Vikki went to the zoo. They stood outside the lion's enclosure and whispered to each other. I'm sure that our lion recognised them too, and let out a big rumbling[4] ROAR of a thank you to his little friends.

Maybe, next time it rains very hard, Lion may come to YOUR house, so remember to give him some freshly baked cake!

**Literary term**

4. This is an example of **onomatopoeia**. The long deep sound made by a lion sounds just like the word 'rumble'.

**In a Nutshell**

**Who** Vikki, Geeti, their mother, and Lion

**Where** A house near a zoo

**What** Lion escaped from the zoo and ate and slept at Vikki and Geeti's house.

**When** After a heavy rain at night

**About the author**

Paro Anand is one of the best Indian writers for children and young adults. She has won the Bal Sahitya Puraskar in 2017 for her anthology *Wild Child and Other Stories*. She also holds a world record for helping over three thousand children make the longest newspaper in the world.

## Comprehension

ia **A. Choose the correct options.**

1. The ______________ filled up with water, so Lion could escape.

   a. cage  b. moat  c. zoo

2. Lion asked the other animals the ______________.

   a. way  b. time  c. date

3. Lion smelled the ____________ in the children's house.
   a. fruits b. meat c. cake
4. ____________ helped to bake the cake.
   a. Geeti and Vikki b. Mom c. Lion
5. The ____________ recognised the children when they visited the zoo.
   a. guard b. lion c. animals
6. The lion slept ________________.
   a. under the bed b. on the table c. in the guard's room

**B. Answer these questions.**

1. Why were Geeti and Vikki upset?
2. How did their mother cheer them up?
3. How did the zoo animals feel during the rain?
4. What did the lion do when he reached the guard?
5. Why did the lion go back to the zoo at dawn?

## Life Skills and Values

kindness to animals

21ST CENTURY Critical Thinking

1. The animals in the zoo were unhappy when it rained. Is it fair to keep animals in the zoo for human entertainment? Share your thoughts.
2. The children did not disturb the lion while he was sleeping. Do you think they were being kind to it?

## Vocabulary

contextual usage

**A. Complete the crossword with words from the story.**

**Across**

2. a place where animals are kept in cages
4. a box made of wires or metal bars in which birds and animals are kept
5. a deep ditch dug around a place
6. an exciting or a dangerous experience

**Down**

1. a short sleep
3. land surrounded by a wall or fence and used for a particular purpose, to keep animals in a zoo

Read this sentence.

The lion **slipped away** at dawn.

Here, *slipped away* is an example of **phrasal verbs**, which are verbs followed by an adverb or a preposition.

**B. Look at these phrasal verbs with *get*. Match them with their meanings.**

| Phrasal verbs | Meanings |
|---|---|
| 1. get through | a. escape |
| 2. get across | b. pass an examination |
| 3. get along with | c. to make someone understand something |
| 4. get away | d. be friendly with someone |
| 5. get into | e. become involved in something |

**C. Now, fill in the blanks with the above phrasal verbs. You may have to change the forms of the verbs.**

1. Don't ______________ a fight, even if you are angry.
2. She is very good at ______________ her ideas to others.
3. The two class monitors ______________ each other quite well.
4. Although she was unwell, she ______________ the entrance exam.
5. The thief ______________ even though the police chased him across the town.

**Grammar** simple future tense

The **simple future tense** talks about an action that will happen in the future. It is also used to talk about future plans. We use *shall/will* + the base form of the verb to get the simple future tense.

**Examples:** The lion **will go** away.

Geeti and Vikki **will visit** the zoo the next day.

**ia A. Fill in the blanks with the simple future tense of the given verbs.**

need go watch visit play buy

1. I ________________ my grandparents next month.
2. I ________________ to the library to search for this book.
3. My parents ________________ me a bicycle for my birthday.
4. Shreya ________________ the football match on TV tomorrow.
5. The brothers ________________ cricket with their friends this weekend.
6. Sheila is going to Shimla next week. She ________________ warm clothes there.

## types of sentences

A **sentence** is a group of words that make complete sense. There are different ways in which we can make sentences.

Most sentences tell us about things or state facts. We use a full stop at the end of these.

**Example:** Everyone stayed at home.

Sentences that are asked to a person to get some information are known as questions. These always end with a question mark.

**Example:** What do they do when it rains?

Sentences that are used to ask somebody to do something politely are called requests. These always end with a full stop or a question mark.

**Examples:** Please pass me the book.
Can you please close the door for me?

Commands are sentences that are used to order or instruct someone to do something. These end in a full stop or an exclamation mark.

**Example:** Finish your food and get ready.

Exclamation marks are also used at the end of sentences that express surprise, shock, happiness, or anger.

**Example:** The lion was free!

**B. Unjumble the words in these sentences.**

1. a dress What lovely!
2. room back to Go the.
3. pen you a Do have red?
4. want I become to a writer.
5. pass the Please salt me to.

**C. Punctuate the sentences correctly depending on their types.**

1. She sings so well
2. What a lovely view
3. Where are you going
4. I have a piano lesson today
5. Sit down and don't make any noise
6. Please put this book back on the shelf

## Study Skills

### Spelling

words ending with *-sion*, *-cian*, and *-tion*

Look at these words.

rev**ision** music**ian** stat**ion**

All three words are pronounced with similar sounds but are spelled differently.

**Add *-sion*, *-cian*, or *-tion* to complete each word given in the box. Write the words in the correct columns.**

physi- magi- atten- direc- confu- deci- reac- explo- electri-

| -sion | -cian | -tion |
| --- | --- | --- |
| | | |

## Listening

listening to announcements and gap filling

**Listen to some announcements and fill in the blanks.**

1. **At the airport**

   Good __________, passengers! This is the __________ announcement.
   Flight Number __________ is going to __________.
   Passengers with __________ and those needing __________ can begin boarding.

2. **At the railway station**

   The __________ Express is arriving from __________.
   The train was supposed to arrive at __________. It is late by __________.
   It will arrive at platform number __________.

## Speaking

talking about a book

Communication Collaboration

**You have read a story written by an Indian author. With the help of your parents or family members, read a story in an Indian language. Then, tell your friends about the story you have read.**

**Useful words and phrases**

I found the story interesting because…

- beautiful pictures
- thrilling plot
- lovable characters
- about fantasy and magic
- about school and friends
- about brave deeds

## Writing

writing a dialogue

Creativity

**Imagine that you are Geeti and you are discussing the night the lion came to your house, with your sister, Vikki. Write suitable dialogues for yourself and Vikki to discuss what happened that night. Be creative and don't forget to use proper punctuation.**

**You can start like this:**

**Geeti:** Remember the night the lion came to our house?
**Vikki:** Oh yes! He ate our cake!
**Geeti:** Did you wake up when he came to our bedroom?

## Explore More

**Read** the story *A Whale of the Wild* by Rosanne Parry. It is about the journey of two orca (large black and white killer whale) siblings who face loss and destruction of their homes.

**Watch** *Free Willy*, which is a film about an orca that swims to freedom with the help of a little boy.

# Project 3

**A. You read about travelling to outer space in the chapters *Kalpana Chawla* and *The Big Beyond*. Imagine that you and your friends are going on a trip to outer space. You will have to stock up your spaceship with everything you need, as you will be away from Earth for six months. What you take will have to last you for the whole period. In groups of four, talk about the following points and present it to the rest of the class.**

Creativity Collaboration

- **Food items you need to carry:** Remember that there is no refrigerator for storing food, so you have to plan carefully. You will not be able to throw anything. So, if you take chocolates, think of what you would do with the wrappers. Make a list of the tinned/canned basic food you should take, along with a few of your favourite snacks.
- **Things you need to carry:** Remember that there are no taps in spaceships for running water. So, plan carefully what clothes and personal items you would need for six months.
- **What are some of the things you would miss the most about Earth?**

**B. You read about physical diversity in the chapters *Earrings for Nina* and *I See What You Miss*. There are many people who may look physically different from us but can succeed even if they might not have two hands, two legs, or both eyes. Such people have fought illnesses and disabilities, like being unable to hear, speak, or see. Find out about any one of the given personalities. Prepare a scrapbook using photos and newspaper reports, and tell their story in class.**

Arunima Sinha

Andrea Boccelli

Nicholas James Vujicic

Stephen Hawking

Louis Braille

**Answers to Self-Assessment given on page 9**

**A.** 1. keep up 2. Cheer up 3. find out 4. put on 5. call off

**B.** 1. seen, scene 2. rode, road 3. blew, blue 4. tale, tail 5. mane, main

**C.** 1. our 2. hers 3. my 4. yours 5. their

**D.** 1. won 2. tells 3. are coming 4. run 5. were standing

**E.** Countable nouns: apple, book, man, seat, computer
Uncountable nouns: blood, sand, oil, sugar, water

**F.** 1. in 2. over 3. between 4. on 5. on